Diadem

Diadem

Selected Poems by
Marosa di Giorgio

Translated from the Spanish
and with an Introduction by
Adam Giannelli

BOA Editions, Ltd. ❖ Rochester, NY ❖ 2012

First Edition

For information about permission to reuse any material from this book, please
contact The Permissions Company at www.permissionscompany.com or e-mail
permdude@eclipse.net.

Publications by BOA Editions, Ltd.—a not-for-profit corporation under section 501
(c) (3) of the United States Internal Revenue Code—are made possible with funds
from a variety of sources, including public funds from the New York State Council
on the Arts, a state agency; the Literature Program of the National Endowment for
the Arts; the County of Monroe, NY; the Lannan Foundation for support of the
Lannan Translations Selection Series; the Mary S. Mulligan Charitable Trust; the
Rochester Area Community Foundation; the Arts & Cultural Council for Greater
Rochester; the Steeple-Jack Fund; the Ames-Amzalak Memorial Trust in memory
of Henry Ames, Semon Amzalak and Dan Amzalak; and contributions from many
individuals nationwide.

Cover Design: Sandy Knight
Cover Art: Barbara Weissberger
Interior Design and Composition: Richard Foerster
Manufacturing: McNaughton & Gunn
BOA Logo: Mirko

Library of Congress Cataloging-in-Publication Data

Di Giorgio, Marosa.
 Diadem : selected poems / by Marosa di Giorgio ; translated by Adam
Giannelli. — 1st ed.
   p. cm. — (Lannan translations selection series ; 22)
 ISBN 978-1-934414-97-2 (pbk. : alk. paper)
 I. Giannelli, Adam. II. Title.
 PQ8520.14.I4D53 2012
 861'.64—dc23
                          2012014245

Lannan

ART WORKS.
arts.gov

BOA Editions, Ltd.
250 North Goodman Street, Suite 306
Rochester, NY 14607
www.boaeditions.org
A. Poulin, Jr., Founder (1938–1996)

State of the Arts

NYSCA

Contents

Introduction

"Her style is very particular; one can recognize it by reading a single line. It doesn't resemble anyone else's," writes César Aira, describing Marosa di Giorgio's work.[1] Di Giorgio has one of the most distinct and recognizable voices in Latin American letters. Her surreal and fable-like prose poems invite comparison to the work of Kafka, Felisberto Hernández, Julio Cortázar, Alejandra Pizarnik, even Lewis Carroll or contemporary American poet Russell Edson, but di Giorgio's voice, imagery, and themes—childhood, the Uruguayan countryside, a perception of the sacred—are her own.

The title of her ninth book, *La liebre de marzo* (The March Hare, 1981), is an homage to the inventive fiction of Lewis Carroll, but also to the wild hare that would "appear and disappear" in the fields of her childhood.[2] Her entire work fuses the fictive and natural worlds. Di Giorgio (1932–2004) was raised outside of the city of Salto in northwestern Uruguay. Her family, immigrants descended from Italian peasants, owned two small farms, and her grandfather, Eugenio Medici, cultivated the land with the help of her father, planting orange and olive trees to recreate the Tuscan countryside. "A pioneer," according to di Giorgio, he made his own wine and even raised silkworms.[3] Her childhood in the countryside profoundly influenced her poems, which all take place in the same imaginary landscape—a farm enveloped by gardens and orchards. The poems revolve around the life of a young girl, similar to the protagonist in *Alice in Wonderland*, who escapes from her mother and family to interact with the surrounding flora and fauna. Throughout her prose fragments, all things—dolls, foxes, butterflies, grandparents—intermingle through endless exchanges that result in both eroticism and brutality.

Mesa de esmeralda (Emerald Tablet, 1985), her tenth book, is named after a text by the alchemist Hermes Trismegistus, an allusion that befits the endless transformations in di Giorgio's poems. One of the tablet's inscriptions states, "That which is above is like to that which is below, and that which is below is like to that which is above," merging the heavens and the earth. Similarly, di Giorgio's poems shun hierarchy and hover at ground level, or slightly above the ground with the leaves and loquats, butterflies and branches. The poems span the whole of experience, fusing the angelic and diabolic, domestic and savage, masculine and feminine, biographic and mythic. Cows debate as if in parliament; beds sprout roots; a hermaphroditic snail ("man and maiden") wanders through the garden; the birth of the speaker's sister summons the three kings. According to Aira, "Marosa di Giorgio's poetic world is made up of transformations, surprises, fluid conduits between the animal and human; it wavers between fairy tale and hallucination, and is ruled by a steadfast courtesy that does not exclude irony or cruelty. In her poems it's not uncommon for the girl who narrates to make love to a horse, or a snail, or a witch, or suddenly lay a large green egg made of rubber, or a small red one of porcelain; to take flight, or die each and every night, or awaken as a spikenard, is perfectly commonplace."[4]

Like Walt Whitman, di Giorgio expanded the same work throughout her career: *Los papeles salvajes* (The Wild Papers), her collected poetry, which unites fourteen books. The collection is comprised of a series of interrelated fragments, and, although many poems consist of narrative flashes, the book lacks a continuous arc. One unlikely event transpires after another. Even though it lacks a sustained storyline, the book is united by a sense of place, albeit imaginary—a house surrounded by violets and magnolia trees, orchards filled with orange blossoms, an elementary school. In addition, a recurring cast of characters, human and inhuman, shuffles in and out—a mother and father, grandparents, a sister named Nidia, cousins, the Virgin Mary, the Devil, butterflies, moles. Since her poems inhabit the same landscape, they can be read as one long meditation. In an interview, di Giorgio described the unity of her work: "It's like a novel…. There isn't a predominant, well-defined plot, like some novels, although nowadays they don't always have one. I think of it as the recreation of a world, and for that reason it has one of the characteristics of a novel. At the same time, it's a poem, since the language is eminently poetic. From one book to another there's no separation. I'm still the same, telling tales, pressing on, steady, tenacious." She described her work as a forest in which she plants more trees—or a fan that always has another fold.[5]

Di Giorgio titled her first book *Poemas* (Poems, 1953), and throughout her life insisted that she wrote poetry, not prose, although a glance at the works themselves, most of which lack lineation, would tempt one to call them prose poems. The expansiveness of prose accommodates her long catalogs of flowers and insects, and captures the lightning speed of the narratives. Russell Edson distinguishes between prose and poetry through their treatment of time: "Time flows *through* prose, and *around* poetry. Poetry is the sense of the permanent, of time held. Prose is the sense of *normal* time, time flowing."[6] If poetry is, in essence, a crystallization, then prose is a condensation, a falling rain. And so these poems present a tempest, not only of pebbles and locusts, but of memories, ghosts, faith, sadness, life, and death. Through prose, di Giorgio registers the erosions of time ("the flowers close forever behind me"), and the dawns within time ("sprouts of grass," an egg hatching with "a rustling of ruffled paper"). The poems, however, are not without stays in the wreckage. New paragraphs designate changes in perspective or slow the poems to a meditative pace. One of the most innovative aspects of her work is how she slips seamlessly from prose into verse, often beginning a paragraph in the middle of a sentence, interrupting the syntax, like a line break. By mingling the fluidity of prose with the concision of verse, she creates a malleable form in which time contracts and expands. It seems fitting that the poem that begins "God's here. / God speaks," about God's presence in the world, casts the domestic scene in prose and the description of God in lines, uniting the eternal and ephemeral.

María Negroni describes di Giorgio's voice as "a language of leaps, which deploys irresolvable phrases, sudden commas, and unexpected shifts in tense."[7] Di Giorgio's punctuation is idiosyncratic, and commas and semicolons pepper her poems. Like Virginia Woolf, she often separates independent clauses with semicolons, which resemble a series of doors flung open by an incessant flow of thought, and her frequent commas, which disregard grammar and jostle the syntax, create a jolting rhythm. For the sake of clarity, I have removed some commas from the translations; however, in replicating her peculiar idiom, in many cases I have retained the original punctuation and run-on sentences. Interestingly, di Giorgio often employs commas to create a double resonance: "I searched for the book, in secret, I leafed through page after page." Does the speaker search for the book in secret? Or leaf through it in secret? The ambiguous punctuation allows for multiple readings, blurring one event with the next and veiling the scene in mystery. Like Lewis Carroll, she is also fond of wordplay, and often disrupts her descriptions with alliteration, neologisms, and near homophones. These slight shifts in sound create a sense of improvisation and draw attention to the words as signifiers, the poem as act. Roberto Echavarren notes, "Due to similar sounds, words sprout one out of the other, like homophonic alternatives, to break or confound the established train of thought."[8] Echavarren cites two examples ("huesos, huevos"; "comedores, corredores"), both of which occur in my translation. It's as if one word morphs into another. Here's my attempt at the latter: "We walked through the dark kitchen doors / corridors." As a translator, I have replicated these verbal effects cautiously, echoing the whimsy of the originals only when it felt natural in English. In the case of "huesos, huevos," my translation—"bones, eggs"—ignores sound altogether, since I felt it was important to balance an image of death with one of birth.

Although di Giorgio never used the title *Diadem* for any of her books, it is the title she chose for a theatrical recital of her poems, which was first performed in the theater La Máscara in Montevideo in 1986. During these performances, di Giorgio, drawing on her background in theater, would recite a selection of poems, which lasted about fifty minutes, from memory. She would enter with a bouquet of carnations, and eventually scatter them across the stage, walking over the flowers in her bare feet. Teresa Porzecanski describes attending one of these recitals: "On the dimly lit stage, and seemingly without feet, as if it had flown there, a figure appears wrapped in a long, black garment, above which glows a mass of red hair, almost the color of carrots. It is a woman.... Her voice is serious, deep, and has what can be called a silky quality."[9] Di Giorgio performed recitals across the globe, including performances in Argentina, Venezuela, Mexico, the United States, Spain, and France. A version of the show was recorded in 1994 and included as a compact disk with the title *Diadema* inside her last book. She explained the origin of the title: "The word *diadem* occurs within the recital, but it's also a garland of poems selected from different books. Therefore it's a kind of diadem."[10] Since she used the title herself for a small selection of her poems, it seems like an appropriate title for this selection.

The title also alludes to the diadem that crowns the Virgin Mary, a recurring image in her poems. Di Giorgio was raised as a Catholic, and the traditions of the Church influence her poetry as much as the rural countryside. Her first poem, she insists, was inspired by an image of the Virgin: "My fascination with the Church arose from cloudy reveries incited by the prayer cards, and through them the Virgin Mary cast a veritable spell over me. I wrote my first poem to her beneath a lemon tree, mixing the fruits, the flowers, the open air and sun, with the white and blue prayer card of the Virgin."[11] The Virgin continually appears throughout her poems, and the diadem serves as an image of authority and femininity. A full circle, it is also a symbol of plenitude, and of eternity.

The Wild Papers, di Giorgio's collected poetry, has been published four times, expanding over the years. The most recent version appeared in 2008, and gathered in a single volume nearly seven hundred pages of poetry. *Diadem* selects from poems over the course of this career, and offers a mere glimpse of her enormous productivity. This selection spans twenty-two years, showcasing poems from her fourth to her eleventh book. Her earliest efforts are comprised of longer narratives, so her fourth book, *Historial de las violetas* (The History of Violets, 1965), serves as an appropriate starting point, marking a shift to more concise and lyric forms. Since *The History of Violets* has already been translated by Jeannine Marie Pitas,[12] I've only included one poem from that collection. The rest of the book continues where *The History of Violets* leaves off, from her fifth book, *Magnolia* (1965), to the last volume of poetry that di Giorgio published as its own book, *La falena* (The Moth, 1987). In 1993 she published *Misales* (Missals), a collection of erotic stories, which began a shift in her career toward longer narratives and more pronounced eroticism. It was followed by two more collections of erotic tales and a novel. Completed shortly before her death, her final book, *La flor de lis* (Fleur de Lis, 2004), culminated her life's work, intermingling narrative, lyricism, and eroticism. During her later years, *The Wild Papers* continued to expand, but less steadily. She produced three more volumes of poetry, which were included at the end of subsequent editions of *The Wild Papers* but weren't published as individual books. The final sequence, an elegy for her grandfather, consists of less than twenty poems. While these final three volumes merit attention, I have not selected from them, focusing instead on the middle of her career.

When asked which was her favorite book, di Giorgio responded, "It's all the same book. I'm writing one book with many sections. Perhaps, *The March Hare*."[13] Because of the cohesion of her work, I did not feel obligated to represent each book equally, and have selected most amply from di Giorgio's confessed favorite. In a career that begins and ends with longer narratives, *The March Hare*, at the midpoint, represents the pinnacle of her lyricism. The poems tend to be more compressed, and I feel that a generous sampling from this book balances the narrative strains that come before and after it. It should also be noted that di Giorgio wrote longer books as her career progressed. *The History of Violets* contains thirty-five poems, while *The March Hare* has approximately one hundred forty, and *The Moth*, two hundred fifty across five sections. The first section of *Diadem*, which groups four books together, reflects this difference. Finally, some of her early books, such as *The History of Violets*, devote a single page to each poem, but as her books grew in length she placed more than one poem on a page, and separated them with numbers or asterisks. The switch was probably a practical one, but the difference in form also slightly alters how one reads the work. Placing each fragment on a page presents them as poems, while the uninterrupted flow of fragment after fragment, especially with the omission of titles, looks more like a work of fiction. Since this is a short selection, I have bestowed on each fragment the dignity of its own page, but the book can also be read from cover to cover as an interrelated series.

When I traveled to Uruguay in August 2011, the poets Leonardo Garet and Myriam Albisu took me to what was left of the di Giorgio family farm. The house that had belonged to her grandfather had been torn down, and there remained only a crumbling pink wall beside a towering palm tree. The other house, which had belonged to her parents, was still standing—white with wood blinds. Since it was still occupied, we never went inside, but walked around and chatted with a blind woman who lived there. It was winter in Uruguay, and half the trees were leafless. A single white horse grazed in the pasture. It was difficult to imagine that this landscape had inspired the fecundity in di Giorgio's poems, but I saw some flowerpots, growing herbs and cacti, beside the house—one in the shape of a swan. And in front grew a garden with bromeliads. A ladder led into a tree, and I could make out a few unripe lemons, hanging, green among the green leaves. A table with four chairs stood in the grass, where a girl might share tea with a doll or hare, or drink a glass of ochre wine and watch a butterfly, or a fairy with crimson dahlia in its hand, flutter through the air. I looked for the Devil tied to a jasmine with a bowl of milk. Even though I knew I wouldn't find him, it was hard not to relate the farm to the poems. As di Giorgio notes, one thing blurs into another: "The five white tips of a lily are the same as the five silver points of a star. It's like a reflection. So the star and lily transform, while remaining a star and a lily..."[14]

NOTES

All English translations are by Adam Giannelli, unless otherwise noted.

1. César Aira, *Diccionario de autores latinoamericanos* (Buenos Aires: Emecé, 2001), 173.

2. Marosa di Giorgio, *No develarás el misterio*, ed. Nidia di Giorgio and Edgardo Russo (Buenos Aires: El Cuenco de Plata, 2010), 40.

3. Ibid., 72.

4. César Aira, *Diccionario de autores latinoamericanos*, 174.

5. Marosa di Giorgio, *No develarás el misterio*, 41, 76.

6. Russell Edson, "The Prose Poem in America," *Parnassus* 5 (1976/77): 322.

7. María Negroni, *Galería fantástica* (Mexico City: Siglo Veintiuno, 2009), 90.

8. Roberto Echavarren, *Marosa di Giorgio: devenir intenso* (Montevideo: Lapzus, 2005), 9.

9. Teresa Porzecanski, "Marosa di Giorgio: Uruguay's Sacred Poet of the Garden," trans. Nancy Abraham Hall, in *A Dream of Light and Shadow: Portraits of Latin American Women*, ed. Marjorie Agosín (Albuquerque: Univ. of New Mexico Press, 1995), 303–04.

10. Quoted in Leonardo Garet, *El milagro incesante* (Montevideo, Aldebarán, 2006), 60.

11. Marosa di Giorgio, *No develarás el misterio*, 43.

12. Marosa di Giorgio, *The History of Violets*, trans. Jeannine Marie Pitas (Brooklyn: Ugly Duckling, 2010).

13. Marosa di Giorgio, *No develarás el misterio*, 147.

14. Ibid., 98.

de Historial de las violetas,
Magnolia,
La guerra de los huertos,
y Está en llamas el jardín natal

from The History of Violets,
Magnolia,
The War of the Orchards,
and The Native Garden Is in Flames

(1965–71)

Los hongos nacen en silencio; algunos nacen en silencio; otros, con un breve alarido, un leve trueno. Unos son blancos, otros rosados, ése es gris y parece una paloma, la estatua a una paloma; otros son dorados o morados. Cada uno trae —y eso es lo terrible— la inicial del muerto de donde procede. Yo no me atrevo a devorarlos; esa carne levísima es pariente nuestra.

Pero, aparece en la tarde el comprador de hongos y empieza la siega. Mi madre da permiso. Él elige como un águila. Ese blanco como el azúcar, uno rosado, uno gris.

Mamá no se da cuenta de que vende a su raza.

The mushrooms are born in silence; some are born in silence; others, with a brief shriek, a bit of thunder. Some are white, others pink, that one's gray and looks like a dove, the statue of a dove; some are gold or purple. Each one bears—and this is the horrible part—the initials of the dead person from which it springs. I don't dare devour them; that tender flesh is our relative.

But in the afternoon the mushroom buyer comes and starts to pick them. My mother lets him. He chooses like an eagle. That one, white as sugar, a pink one, a gray one.

Mama doesn't realize she's selling her own kind.

A veces, los caballos se reúnen allá. Las lechuzas con sus sobretodos oscuros, sus lentes muy fuertes, sus campanillas extrañas, convocan a los hongos blancos como huesos, como huevos. A veces, tenemos hambre y no hay un animalillo que degollar.

Entonces, vamos por la escalera, hacia el desván, a buscar las viejas piñas, los racimos de tabla con sus uvas duras y oscuras, las viejas almendras; al partirlas, salta la bicheja, lisa, suave, nacarada, rosa o azul; si es de color oro, la arrojamos al aire y ella se pone a girar envuelta en un anillo de fuego, como un planeta.

A veces, ni tengo hambre. La luna está fija con sus plumas veteadas. Cantan los caballos.

Sometimes, the horses gather over there. The owls, with their dark overcoats, thick spectacles, and strange little bells, summon the mushrooms, white as bones, as eggs. Sometimes, we go hungry without a little animal to slaughter.

So we climb the steps to the attic, searching for old pineapples, clusters of grapes, wooden and dark, old almonds; when we crack them open, the creature leaps out of hiding, smooth, soft, nacreous, pink or blue; if it's gold, we fling it into the air where it starts to spin enveloped by a ring of flames, like a planet.

Sometimes, I'm not even hungry. The moon perches with its marbled feathers. The horses sing.

Dios está aquí.

Dios habla.

A veces en la noche, cuando menos espero, de entre las cosas, sale su cara, su frente, inmensa y diminuta como una estrella. Centelleante y fija.

Hace años que anda por la casa.

Allá en la infancia yo no me atreví a decirlo a nadie; ni a papá, ni a mamá; era como un cordero, una forma pavorosa, que se comía las hierbas, bramaba un poco, topaba la casa.

Una gallina blanca como la muerte,
como la nieve; o negra;
una gallina crucificada con las alas bien abiertas,
y el cuello manando sangre.

Él estuvo presente en la fiesta que dio mi madre –no sé por qué–.

Cuando vinieron todas sus amigas –de collares y coronas– y se sentaron en las habitaciones, y se les servía miel, vino, manzanas, otras confituras, nadie se fijó en un comensal de ojos inmóviles y grises.

Dios vuela un poco;
a veces, cruza volando la noche,
como si fuera a irse.

God's here.

God speaks.

Sometimes at night, when I least expect it, his face, his forehead, emerges among our things, massive and tiny as a star. Shimmering and motionless.

For years he has gone about the house.

Back in childhood I didn't dare tell anyone; not papa, or mama; he was like a lamb, a terrifying shape, that would eat up the grass, bleat a little, and ram into the house.

A hen white as death,

white as snow; or black;

a hen crucified with its wings wide open,

its neck spurting blood.

He attended the party my mother gave—I don't know why—.

When all her friends came—wearing necklaces and tiaras—and sat in the rooms, and were served honey, wine, apples, other confections, no one noticed a guest with glazed gray eyes.

God flies a little;

sometimes, he flies across the night,

as if he were leaving.

Ahora, estamos otra vez, en el interior de la casa; miro los gozosos muebles. Papá dice que, por algunos meses, la guerra sólo será una suave guerrilla; se oyen rumores en el horizonte; día a día, choques, que no producen ni producirán ningún muerto. Mi pavor disminuye. Además, aquéllos han prometido ayudarle. La subgente aderezará para él, cazos de hierro, de cerámica, y la gran carroza guerrera, donde un día, el del encuentro final, él desfile como el gran duque de las hierbas. Y así me entero, que, lo que está en juego, también, es la corona de los huertos.

Recorro los muebles, las dulceras, tan bellas, colmadas y vacías, color oro, color rosa.

Casi nunca, vienen visitas a casa. Hoy, unos amigos del norte, de la zona de alianza. Están en el jardín, con la abuela, mamá y el fijo abuelo; se habla de la guerra, se miente un poco. Se les invita con miel. Somos colmeneros. Esta miel parece higo, parece azahar, y tiene un fulgor increíble. Pero, las mariposas y los pájaros se ilusionan, creen que la mesa está puesta para ellos, e intervienen en la conversación, la interrumpen, se paran en el borde de los vasos, hay que dejarles; luego, se marean, y algunos no pueden irse; borrachos y radiantes, giran allí, se fosilizan, se abrillantan, crean su propia órbita, sus anillos. Tenemos algunas constelaciones en el jardín.

Now, we're inside the house again; I look at the cheerful furniture. Papa says that, for a few months, the war will reduce to a gentle uprising; we hear rumbles in the distance; day by day, clashes that don't produce or won't produce a single casualty. My fear subsides. Besides, they've promised to help him, the people underground. They're going to prepare for him, iron pans, ceramic ones, and the great war carriage, where one day, after the last battle, he'll parade like the great duke of the grasslands. And I realize that what's at stake, as well, is the crown of the orchards.

I walk around the furniture, the candy dishes, so lovely, filled and empty, gold, pink.

We hardly ever have visitors. Today, some friends from the north, the allied zone. They're in the garden, with grandmother, mama, and grandfather, at rest; they talk of the war, exaggerate a little. They're offered honey. We're beekeepers. This honey tastes like figs, orange blossoms, and has an incredible luster. But the butterflies and birds delude themselves, they think that the table has been set for them, and intrude into the conversation, interrupt it, they land on the rims of the glasses, we let them be; then they get dizzy, and can't fly away; drunk and shining, they spin in circles, they fossilize, crystallize, they create their own orbits, their rings. We have some constellations in the garden.

Anoche, volvió, otra vez, La Sombra; aunque ya, habían pasado cien años, bien la reconocimos. Pasó el jardín de violetas, el dormitorio, la cocina; rodeó las dulceras, los platos blancos como huesos, las dulceras con olor a rosa. Tornó al dormitorio, interrumpió el amor, los abrazos; los que estaban despiertos, quedaron con los ojos fijos; los que soñaban, igual la vieron. El espejo donde se miró o no se miró, cayó trizado. Parecía que quería matar a alguno. Pero, salió al jardín. Giraba, cavaba, en el mismo sitio, como si debajo estuviese enterrado un muerto. La pobre vaca, que pastaba cerca de las violetas, se enloqueció, gemía como una mujer o como un lobo. Pero, La Sombra se fue volando, se fue hacia el sur. Volverá dentro de un siglo.

Last night, again, the Shadow returned; although a hundred years had passed, we recognized it instantly. It went past the violet garden, the bedroom, the kitchen; it circled the candy dishes, the plates white as bone, the candy dishes smelling of roses. It went back to the bedroom, interrupted love, embraces; those who were awake stared, transfixed; those dreaming still saw it. The mirror, where it saw or didn't see itself, shattered to the floor. It seemed as if it wanted to kill someone. But it fled to the garden. It was digging, whirling, in the same place, as if a body were buried below. The poor cow, grazing by the violets, was going mad, moaning like a woman or a wolf. But the Shadow flew away, flew to the south. It'll return in a century.

Recuerdo mi casamiento, realizado remotamente; allá en los albores del tiempo.

Mi madre y mis hermanas se iban por los corredores. Y los viejos murciélagos —testigos de las nupcias de mis padres— salieron de entre las telarañas, a fumar, descreídos, sus pipas.

Todo el día surgió humo de la casa; pero, no vino nadie; sólo al atardecer empezaron a acudir animalejos e increíbles parientes, de las más profundas chacras; muchos de los cuales sólo conocíamos de nombre; pero, que habían oído la señal; algunos con todo el cuerpo cubierto de vello, no necesitaron vestirse, y, caminaban a trechos en cuatro patas. Traían canastillas de hongos de colores: verdes, rojos, dorados, plateados, de un luminoso amarillo, unos crudos; otros, apenas asados o confitados.

El ceremonial exigía que todas las mujeres se velasen —sólo se les asomaban los ojos, y parecían iguales—; y que yo saliera desnuda, allí bajo las extrañas miradas.

Después, sobre nuestras cabezas, nuestros platos, empezaron a pasar carnes chisporroteantes y loco vino. Pero, bajo tierra, la banda de tamboriles, de topociegos, seguía sordamente.

A la medianoche, fui a la habitación principal.

Antes de subir al coche, me puse el mantón de las mujeres casadas. Los parientes dormían, deliraban. Como no había novio me besé yo misma, mis propias manos.

Y partí hacia el sur.

I remember my wedding, which took place far away, at the white dawn of time.

My mother and sisters were walking through the halls. And the old bats—who witnessed my parents' vows—emerged, incredulous, from the spider webs to smoke their pipes.

All day smoke rose from the house; but no one came; it wasn't until dusk that little critters and incredible relatives started to arrive, from the furthest farms, many of whom we only knew by name, but who had heard the signal; some were covered head to foot with hair, they didn't need to wear clothes, and walked here and there on all fours. They brought baskets of colorful mushrooms: green, red, gold, silver, bright yellow, some raw; others, lightly roasted or sweetened.

The ceremony dictated that all the women put on veils—only their eyes were visible and they all looked alike—and that I walk before them naked, there beneath those strange glances.

Then, over our heads, our plates, they began to pass sizzling steaks and intoxicating wine. But, underground, the drum band, the blindmoles, kept beating faintly.

At midnight I went to the master bedroom.

Before climbing into the carriage, I put on the shawl that married women wear. The relatives muttered in their sleep. Since there wasn't a groom, I kissed myself, my own hands.

And headed south.

Ayer conocí el nombre secreto de mi casa.

Era ya el atardecer, y todos paseaban, por la huerta, el jardín, la calleja, donde las coliflores levantaban sus hermosas puntas y tazas de plata. Ya ardía alguna estrella, algún cometa y su cabello fatídico.

Entonces, tomé la lámpara, la más pequeña, y fui, en puntas de pie, hasta el armario. Busqué el libro, sigilosamente, pasé hoja por hoja; hasta que, todo empezó a temblar como si estuviera por llegar la muerte, y todo se quedó inmóvil como si ya hubiese llegado.

Y yo la vi, no la rosa encarnada que estás imaginando, ni rosa, ni amarilla, ni una efectista rosa negra. Sólo un pimpollo plano y claro, de pocos pétalos.

Parece de agua, una gema de mármol, parece un lirio.

Pero, Rosa es el nombre secreto de mi raza.

La tarde caía como si fuera un siglo.

Yesterday I discovered the secret name of my house.

It was already dusk, and everyone was strolling through the orchard, the garden, the narrow path, where the cauliflower lifted its splendid tips and silver cups. Already a star was burning, a comet with its ominous hair.

So I grabbed the lamp, the smallest one, and went, on tiptoes, to the armoire. I searched for the book, in secret, I leafed through page after page; until everything started to tremble as if death were about to arrive, and everything froze as if death had already arrived.

And I saw it, not the blood-red rose you're imagining, not pink, or yellow, or a sensational black rose. Only a bud, flat and clear, with a few petals.

It seemed to be made of water, a marble gem, a lily.

But Rosa is the secret name of my kind.

The afternoon was falling as if it were a century.

de Clavel y tenebrario

from Carnation and Tenebrae Candle

(1979)

Quisiera contar cómo nacían las cosas.

Cuando ocupábamos aquella vivienda, que no tenía nada de particular. Casi nada. Con sus numerosas alcobas en las que hacíamos representaciones, que los vecinos espiaban por todas las puertas y ventanas. En uno de esos habitáculos –pero, uno sin techo y sin piso–, desde la tierra, a veces, desde la noche hasta el alba, nacían las cosas: cubiertos, ralladores, platos, ollas, tazas. Todo allí, pulcro, tierno y casi tembloroso. Lo llevábamos a la cocina para utilizarlo, y nunca se nos ocurrió hacer negocio.

Y cuando nos mudamos a otra vivienda tampoco nadie comentó nada.

Lo cuento, ahora, que, ya, parece un cuento.

I'd like to tell how things were born.

When we lived in that house that had nothing distinguishing about it. Almost nothing. With its many bedrooms where we put on performances, which the neighbors spied on through the doors and windows. In one of those quarters—but one without a roof or floor—from the earth, sometimes, from night until dawn, things were born: silverware, box graters, plates, pots, cups. All of it there, clean, tender and almost shivering. We brought it to the kitchen to use, and we never thought to profit from it.

And when we moved to another house no one mentioned it then either.

I tell it now since it seems already like a tale.

Hacíamos representaciones en los jardines, a la caída de la tarde, junto a los cedros y las algarrobas; la obra era improvisada, ahí mismo, y yo, siempre, tenía miedo de perder la letra, aunque, nunca, ocurrió tal cosa. Íbamos, de aquí para allá, entre los cedros y los naranjos, y acudían a espiarnos, a escucharnos, los habitantes de todas las casonas vecinas.

También, teníamos algunos animales en el elenco; habían aprendido a moverse en un escenario, a vestirse, a calzarse, y hasta decían algunas palabras.

Desde los doce a los veinte años, representé en todos los jardines.

Pero, después, todo se deshizo.

Y los animales volvieron al bosque a continuar su vida silenciosa.

We would put on plays in the gardens, at twilight, beside the cedar and carob trees; the show was improvised on the spot, and I was always afraid I wouldn't know what to say, although that never happened. We went, back and forth, between the cedar and orange trees, and the neighbors left their houses to come spy on us, to listen to us.

We also had some animals in the cast; they had learned to move across the stage, to dress up, to put on shoes, and they even spoke a few words.

As a teenager, I performed in all the gardens.

But then everything fell apart.

And the animals returned to the forest to resume their silent lives.

Una vez, en casa, nació un caballo, o en los alrededores de la casa; desde el momento de su nacimiento y el de caminar, que casi fueron uno, demostró gran masculinidad y belleza; era azul, reluciente, y la cola le llegaba al suelo. Pero, cuando pasó el tiempo, su color fue tomando otro sentido, y fue como la "flor de un día", ese lirio que dura sólo un día, y que es blanco y con manchas negras; pero, al tocar la plena juventud, ya, estaba totalmente nevado, y así, las opiniones se dividieron; hubo partidarios del caballo negro, y otros, de éste, del de ahora. Las niñas de la casa, que éramos tres, estábamos enamoradas de él, y también, las de las vecinas. Algunas le seguían llamando "el caballo negro", aunque, ya destellase; otras ni siquiera lo nombrábamos. Se alimentaba de ramas, de rosas y alhelíes, y de las cajas de masas que, a propósito, le dejábamos entre los pastos, envueltas, siempre, en papel de color de rosa, que él apartaba desdeñosamente, comiéndose la dorada confitura. Iba y venía, mirándonos con indiferencia, y hasta con burla.

Pasó mucho tiempo. No sé en verdad lo que pasaba. Pero, por verle, abandonamos la canastilla de los estudios y el canasto de las puntillas; no nos imaginábamos ninguna cosa de la vida, en que no estuviese presente aquel caballo.

....

Hasta, que, al final, él se casó con una de nosotras. La que era algo mayor; una muy pálida y de pelo largo.

Recuerdo el día de la boda,

el viaje y el olvido.

Once, in the house, a horse was born, or in the vicinity of the house; from the moment he was born and the moment he started to walk, which were almost the same, he displayed great virility and beauty; he was blue, sleek, and his tail touched the ground. But, as time went on, his color started to take on a different meaning, and he was like the "daylily," that flower that lasts only a day, that's white with black spots; but, when he reached the prime of his youth, his whole body was snow white, and then the opinions diverged; there were those in favor of the black horse, and others, of this one, the one at hand. The girls in the house, all three of us, were in love with him, as were the neighboring girls. Some still called him "the black horse," although now he twinkled; others of us didn't call him anything at all. He fed on branches, roses, and stocks, and boxes of pastries that we left especially for him in the grass, wrapped, always, in pink paper, which he removed disdainfully, consuming the golden filling. He would come and go, watching us indifferently, even mocking us.

Time went on. I wasn't really sure what was going on. But, for a glimpse of him, we'd set aside the little basket of schoolbooks and the big basket of lace; we couldn't imagine anything in the world that didn't include that horse.

....

Until, finally, he married one of us. The one who was a bit older; who was very pale with long hair.

I remember the wedding,

their departure, and the forgetting.

Sí, tal vez, anduviese errada. La solución sería comerme una mariposa. Agoté las otras posibilidades —la dificultad iba a estar en darle caza—; no sé hacer ningún trabajo, no me gusta hacer ningún trabajo. Cruzo, lentamente, la habitación; bajo la pequeña escalera, miro los muebles, erguidos y oscuros. Abro y cierro la puerta. Voy al cantero de los malvones; las anchas hojas son propicias. Tiendo la mano como un garfio, pero, levemente. La mariposa diurna no sirve, es muy tenue; sería como querer cortar la sed con un poco de rocío. La mariposa de la noche es muy especial; es espesa, muy gruesa; todo comible: ojos, patas, alas; todo. Su gusto, a veces, algo deplorable; otras, no, a hierbas, a carnecita. De todos modos, ¿cómo nace una mariposa? ¿Un huevecito sobre una "flor de un día"? ¿sobre un lirio? Se entreabre, deja salir la monja, el muertecillo. Creo que en un mañana, ya, se vuelve adulta y empieza a rodar sobre las flores. Ése debe ser el proceso. Sobre las mariposas nocturnas guardo, es verdad, ciertas inquietudes. Pero, más vale no pensar. Oh, Dios! Ya cayó! Mientras, elucubraba todo esto, ya cayó. Es grande, casi como un pájaro; es "beige" con los alones negros; si… un poco monstruosa; pero, también, se parece a Santa Teresita; la aferré bien. La voy a comer viva. Da miedo matarla.

Yes, perhaps, I was mistaken. The solution would be to eat a butterfly. I exhausted all the other options (the hard part would be chasing after it); I can never go through with anything; I don't like to go through with anything. Slowly, I cross the room; I walk down the short staircase and look at the furniture standing in the dark. I open and close the door. I go to the bed of geraniums; the wide leaves bode well. I extend my hand like a hook, but slowly. The daytime butterfly won't do, it's too light; it'd be like trying to quench thirst with a few drops of dew. The night butterfly is very special; it's firm, plump, entirely edible: eyes, legs, wings; all of it. Sometimes, it tastes wretched; other times, it doesn't; it's like herbs, fresh meat. But how is a butterfly born, anyway? A tiny egg on a "daylily"? a flower? It cracks open, lets out the nun, the little carcass. I think it only takes one morning for it to become an adult and fly around and about the flowers. That must be the process. Towards nocturnal butterflies, I admit, I harbor some reservations. But it's best not to think of it. Oh, God! It just fell! While I was musing on all this, it fell. It's big, almost like a bird; it's beige with wide black wings; perhaps... a bit monstrous; but at the same time it looks like little Saint Teresa; I've snared it. I'm going to eat it alive. I'm afraid to kill it.

Hay diversos tipos de diablas. Las llamadas "catalinas" son de ojos azules y pestañas muy largas; las "teresitas" usan mantón marrón. Se embarazan muy fácilmente; seguido, se ven nuevas camadas de diablos; por todos lados aparecen sus nidadas. Los hijos pequeños vuelan por los cielos altísimos y por el suelo; vuelan y brillan, cubiertos de papel de bombón, papeles de estrella.

Ya, conté que mi abuela ponía tramperos y los cazaba a centenares.

Por años comimos guisado de diablo.

Quisiera explicar el fascinante gusto y es muy difícil; una fragancia a muerto mechado con diamelas.

There are different kinds of she-devils. The ones called "catalinas" have blue eyes and long lashes; the "teresitas" wear brown shawls. They get pregnant very easily; one after another, new litters of devils are born; their broods are everywhere. The young ones fly through the highest skies and skim the ground; they fly and shimmer, encased in candy wrappers, starry paper.

I've already told how my grandmother would set traps and catch them by the hundreds.

For years we ate devil stew.

I wish I could explain its irresistible flavor and it's very difficult; the scent of a dead body larded with jasmine.

Las langostas venían del Paraguay; cada una parecía hecha en un leve hueso, en una cáscara; como una catarata, un aluvión, se desmoronaban desde las selvas del cielo. Todos salían a luchar contra ellas. Papá, los abuelos, los propietarios de todas las casonas vecinas, los peones y los perros, usando grandes máscaras de las que colgaban barbas y lamparitas, trajes de luces, como si fueran a torear; salían, así, a espantarlas, usaban ollas y juguetes. Ponían un monigote en cada jardín, en cada almácigo; defendían todas las plantas y cada planta. Cometían grandes locuras y barullos.

Pero, las langostas, igual, se devoraban todo, minuciosamente, fugazmente. Y, también, hacían nidales por todos lados y ponían huevos. Y de noche, se oía un ruido raro; como si se rieran.

Las langostas caían dentro de todo, en la sopa, en las sábanas, en la misa.

Se cerraban las escuelas.

Los niños no sabíamos qué hacer; a veces, cazábamos una y la cortábamos por la mitad.

The locusts came from Paraguay; each one seemed sheathed in a soft bone, a husk; like a waterfall, a deluge, they came tumbling down from the forests in the sky. Everyone ran out to face them. Papa, my grandparents, the owners of all the houses nearby, the farmhands and hounds, wearing huge masks with trailing beards and little dangling lamps, matador suits, as if they were off to fight a bull; they would run out, dressed that way, to scare off the locusts, they used pots and toys. They placed a straw man in every garden, every seedbed; they defended each and every plant. They caused such havoc, such a racket.

But the locusts still devoured everything, thoroughly, swiftly. And they made nests everywhere and laid eggs. And at night, a strange noise could be heard; as if they were laughing.

The locusts fell into everything, into the soup, the sheets, the morning mass.

The schools closed down.

None of us children knew what to do; sometimes, we'd catch one and chop it in half.

Dictaminaron las crucifixiones.

Una muñeca, la de ojos grandes y pestañas largas, que estaba tiesa en su caja azul. (Pero, —yo decía—, la muñeca se volverá a tejer, enseguida);

una begonia, de arterias granates. (Pero, la begonia resucita desde una sola hoja);

un gato ¿cuál? ¿El pequeño, de ojos como de loza que comía carnecita rosada? ¿o el grande, color gris perla, de rostro casi cuadrado, que hacía tantos años que nos acompañaba, y que, a veces, con su mano de felpa entreabría las cazuelas?

¿Eligieron el grande porque, ya, había vivido muchos años?

También, un miembro de la familia.

Papá, mamá, mi hermana o yo.

Papá, dijo, enseguida: Yo voy.

Se hizo un silencio inmenso.

La muñeca fue hincada en una cruz azul; perdió sus celajes.

La begonia quedó todo plateada y arrugada.

El ave —que me olvidé de mencionar— fue clavada por las alas; entreabrió el pico, puso un huevo roto.

El gato tuvo un rostro casi humano, lloró lágrimas de sangre.

Se hizo un silencio inmenso.

Papá, desde la cruz, nos miraba.

Nosotras lo mirábamos como a través de un vidrio.

De las nubes blancas caía nieve, soplaba el viento.

They decreed the crucifixions.

A doll, with round eyes and long lashes, perfectly upright in her blue box. (But—I was saying—the doll can be sewn right back together);

a begonia, with crimson arteries. (But begonias can propagate from a single leaf);

a cat, which one? The little one, with eyes like fine china who would eat scraps of pink meat? or the big one, the color of a gray pearl, with an almost square face, who kept us company for years, and who, sometimes, with her plush paw pried open the pots?

Did they choose the big one since it had lived for so long?

And a member of the family.

Papa, mama, my sister or me.

Papa, right away, said, "I'll go."

A long silence fell.

The doll was fixed to a blue cross; she lost her azure wisps.

The begonia turned silver and shriveled.

The bird—which I forgot to mention—was nailed through the wings; its beak parted, it laid a cracked egg.

The cat had a nearly human expression, it shed tears of blood.

A long silence fell.

Papa, from the cross, looked down at us.

We looked up at him as if through a piece of glass.

From the white clouds, snow was falling, the wind blew.

Luna, estás brillando, otra vez; tu hermosura es tal que se te cae como un río; no hay adjetivo que te quede bien. Soy tu adoradora, tu sonámbula; la noche del día de mi nacimiento debiste brillar insigne como una reina en todo el cielo. Y me elegiste, me embrujaste. No puedo dejar estos ropajes, esta sábana. Estos tules no tienen salida. Eres la única ciudad que quisiera visitar, la única ciudad en la que podría vivir. Foco fijo sobre la infancia; manejaste los duraznеros, que en la noche se colmaban de pequeños sexos rojos y su lúbrico cuchicheo no nos dejaba dormir; promovías la marea de las liebres. Eres el Cine, tus siniestras fotografías, tu blanco y negro, podrían quitar la vida.

Haces nacer mariposas altas y de cabello largo como yo; y mariposas velludas y vacunas, y mariposas en los puentes; deja de poner huevos; siempre estás allí con tus diamelas. No se puede caminar con tanto lirio. Murciélago. Campanario. Aprendí todo lo que haces, a volar sin alas, a usar antifaces, a pasar, siempre, el mismo camino.

No quisiera morir sólo por no dejar de verte.

Aunque sé que has de subir, más tremenda y sola,

de detrás de los muros de la muerte.

Moon, you're shining again; your allure falls from you like a river; no adjective can capture it. I'm your pilgrim, your sleepwalker; on the night I was born you must have shone eminently like a queen in the sky. And you chose me, bewitched me. I can't leave these robes, this sheet. There's no way out of this tulle. You're the only city I'd like to visit, the only city where I could live. Fixed beam over my childhood; you held sway over the peach trees, which at night would fill with tiny red pudenda, and their lewd whispers wouldn't let us sleep; you roused the tides of hares. You're the Movies, your wicked photographs, your black and white, could rob someone of her life.

You give life to tall butterflies with hair as long as mine; and fuzzy bovine butterflies, and butterflies on bridges; please stop laying eggs; you're always there with your jasmine. It's impossible to carry so many lilies. Bat. Belfry. I learned it all from you, to fly without wings, to wear masks, to always travel across the same path.

I ask not to die only so that I don't cease to see you.

Although I know you must rise, more daring and alone,

from behind the walls that keep the dead.

Maté a mamá. Al fin lo hice.

Me senté junto a las pálidas niñas –Nidia, Iris–. Desde los naranjos caía un arroz continuo. Palabras extrañas, "Piedad", "Merced", nos golpeaban en la frente. Pensábamos en magnolias y papeles de organza. Oíamos los trinos de todos los pájaros del naranjal. Al fin, la representación que tuvo origen en mi nacimiento había terminado, la verdad que parecía mentira. Intentamos jugar un poco. Corrimos. Peinamos una muñeca; dos; las tres muñecas. Hasta que cayó la noche; caía la noche. Allá, por el cielo, Mamá, de vestido rojo y sombrero rojo, navegaba contra su voluntad.

I killed my mother. At last I did it.

I sat beside the pale girls—Nidia, Iris—. From the orange trees rice fell perpetually. Strange words, "Mercy," "Grace," struck us on the forehead. We thought about the magnolias and the organza. We heard all the birds in the orange grove trilling. Finally, the performance that began the day I was born had ended, the truth that seemed like a lie. We tried to play. We ran around. We combed a doll's hair; two; three dolls. Until night fell; night was falling. Up above, across the sky, Mama, in a red dress and red hat, was drifting against her will.

de La liebre de marzo

from The March Hare

(1981)

Virgen María, enorme ala sobre toda la niñez y todo el campo. Rosaura plena, azul, rosada, con una estrella en el medio. Palma que se abanica sola, de este a oeste, de sur a norte, pasaba su vestido enorme bordeado de camelias; los huevos y los jazmines le pertenecían. En la noche ardió como una niñita azul, como una lámpara.

Nos despertaba; en sueños, la veíamos, volaba; era la luna.

Pero, bajo su blancura de almendra y nieve, degollaron vacas y corderos, murieron las palomas, los abuelos. No sé;

ahora, la miro, allá distante, como a la rosa, como al laurel.

Virgin Mary, enormous wing over my whole childhood and the whole countryside. Rosaura, blue, pink, luminous, with a star in the middle. Palm that fans itself, from east to west, south to north, her enormous dress drifts, trimmed with camellias; the eggs and jasmine were hers. At night she burned like a blue baby girl, like a lamp.

She'd wake us up; in our dreams, we saw her, flying; she was the moon.

But under her snowy and almond white, cattle and sheep were slaughtered, the doves died, my grandparents. I can't say;

now I see her, there in the distance, like a rose, a laurel.

Para cazar insectos y aderezarlos, mi abuela era especial.

Les mantenía la vida por mayor deleite y mayor asombro de los clientes y convidados.

A la noche, íbamos a las mesitas del jardín con platitos y saleros.

En torno, estaban los rosales; las rosas únicas, inmóviles y nevadas.

Se oía el run run de los insectos, debidamente atados y mareados.

Los clientes llegaban como escondiéndose.

Algunos pedían luciérnagas, que era lo más caro. Aquellas luces.

Otros, mariposas gruesas, color crema, con una hoja de menta y un minúsculo caracolillo.

Y recuerdo cuando servimos a aquella gran mariposa negra, que parecía de terciopelo, que parecía una mujer.

My grandmother had a rare talent for catching insects and seasoning them.

For the distinct pleasure and amazement of her patrons and guests, she would keep them alive.

At night we'd go to the tables in the garden with little plates and saltshakers.

Around us, stood rosebushes; the roses like no others, snow-white and perfectly still.

We could hear the hum hum of the insects, properly bound and dazed.

The patrons came as if out of hiding.

Some asked for fireflies, which were the most expensive. Those lights.

Others, plump butterflies, cream-colored, served with a mint leaf and a tiny snail.

And I remember when we served that great black butterfly, who looked velvet, who looked like a woman.

Un río muy delgado, –lo saltaban los niños–, partía la huerta. A su vera, manzanos de San Juan, manzanas casi blancas, casi celestes, los frutos angélicos.

A la medianoche, desnuda, me levanté; estaba dormida, y veía, todo, como si fuera de día. Además, las plantas de ese jardín, conservaban, en la sombra, sus colores. Así, divisé margaritas, los pimpollos de rosa, rojos como sangre, el gladiolo que hervía como un farol. Recibí el olor de las frutas, pero, no podía detenerme. Tomé la senda. A mi lado pasaban yuyos: salvia, mentas, aralias. Mentas, aralias, hojas, yuyos. Llegué al extremo.

Allá, lejos, y ahí, cerca, él se presentó, sombrío, inmóvil, siempre el mismo, desde remotos siglos.

Desesperada, corté una rama, la sostuve como vistiéndome. Por un instante, creí que iba a volar, a despertar. Pero, todo fue inútil. Con un breve grito, aconteció, otra vez.

A narrow river—the children would jump across it—divided the orchard. Along its banks, San Juan apple trees, apples almost white, almost sky blue, angelic fruits.

At midnight, naked, I got up; I was sleeping, and saw, everything, as if it were daylight. The plants in that garden also kept, in the shadows, their colors. So I spied daisies, blood-red rosebuds, a gladiolus burning up like a lantern. I took in the fragrance of the fruit, but I couldn't linger. I went down the path. At my sides, wild herbs went by: sage, mint, aralia. Mint, aralia, leaves, herbs. I reached the far end.

There, faraway, and there, nearby, he appeared, somber, perfectly still, the same as always, from distant centuries.

Desperate, I broke off a branch. I held it as if I were getting dressed. For a moment, I thought I was going to fly away, or wake up. But it all was useless. With a brief cry, it happened again.

En la tarde estaba en el pasto hablando con Amelia. Amelia tenía ojos celestes, rodeados de oscuro, vestido de organdí amarillo; la falda con tres volados.

Corté algunas manzanas; rápidamente, hice una ensalada de menta, que no se probó.

Pasaban los pastores de la caída de la tarde, con la pica al hombro. Decían por mí: —Ahí está con su muñeca. Es más grande que ella. O casi.

Amelia tenía ojos oscuros, volados dorados. Parecía, de nuevo, inquirir, ansiosa. Expliqué que no podía decirle nada. Que, tal vez, todo aquello fuera mentira, que figuraba en los libros como cuando no es cierto. Sus ojos semejaron brillar de lágrimas.

Entonces, llamé al último pastor; dije el secreto.

El pastor le ordenó algo. Ella obedeció. Él decía "Parece viva".

Lo que ocurrió fue hermosísimo y horrible.

Yo miraba, fijamente, y no miraba. Él se alejó, primero. Después, yo, también, seguí hacia la casa, como si fuera a contarlo.

Sólo Amelia quedó tendida, allá, y aún se le movían las alas doradas.

In the afternoon I sat in the pasture talking with Amelia. Amelia had blue eyes, that darkened at the edges, a yellow organdy dress; the skirt with three ruffles.

I sliced some apples; quickly, I made a mint salad, which was left untouched.

The shepherds walked by at twilight, with their staffs on their shoulders. They said, "There she sits with her doll. It's bigger than her. Or just about."

Amelia had dark eyes, gold ruffles. She seemed, again, to wonder, anxious. I explained I couldn't tell her anything. That, perhaps, it were all a lie, that it appeared in books like other things that aren't true. Her eyes seemed to shine with tears.

So I called over the last shepherd, and told the secret.

The shepherd gave her an order. She obeyed. He was saying, "It's like she's alive."

What happened next was beautiful and horrible.

I watched, transfixed, and didn't watch. He walked away, first. Then I did, too, all the way to the house, as if I were going to tell.

Only Amelia was left, lying there—her gold wings still quivering.

Entre los gladiolos en flor ponía la Virgen su cara celeste; mamá, que andaba cortando tallos, cuidaba de no tocarla; yo, que la seguía, veía que en los jardines vecinos, estaban, también, la Virgen y los pimpollos.

Mamá hizo ramos enormes, desmesurados, y los puso muy arriba y en el suelo.

Y, después, empezó a componer las ensaladas, de colores ardientes, les echaba rocío.

Pero, la mañana no avanzaba, estaba como suspendido el corazón. Hasta que ardieron, de golpe, las Vírgenes-muñecas, los gladiolos, los platos se doblaban en colores, palidecían los vecinos, murió mamá, morí.

Se hizo un silencio inmenso.

Y, nunca, nada de aquello, reapareció.

Between the gladioli in bloom the Virgin set her sky-blue face; mama, cutting stalks, was careful not to touch it; I, following her, could see that the Virgin and the buds were also in the neighboring gardens.

Mama made large, boundless bouquets, and set them up high and on the ground.

And then she started to arrange salads, of burning colors, she sprinkled them with dew.

But the morning stalled, it was as if the heart adjourned. Until, all of a sudden, up in flames went the Virgin-dolls, the gladioli, the plates crumpled in colors, the neighbors faded, mama died, I died.

A long silence fell.

And none of it ever reappeared.

La arboleda luctuosa giraba como el mar. Cayó lluvia. Sobre la calle quedaron unas piedras, chicas, y otras más grandes; eran muchísimas; parecían pedazos de estrellas.

Brillaban con furia, con desesperación. Creía que se iban a ir como liebres; y no se iban.

Entré corriendo; pero, todo era distinto. Los roperos, abiertos. Los santos ¡sin marco, y de pie!

Un pajarillo totalmente azul volaba, siempre, en el mismo lugar, al alcance de mi mano; no lo pude espantar ni cazar.

Se me cayó la trenza, se me cayó el vestido, cayeron las azucenas y la taza.

Quedé prendida a no sé qué,
y a nada.

The dark grove tossed like the sea. Rain was falling. Little stones were left in the street, and large ones; there were many of them, like bits of stars.

They shone furiously, desperately. I thought they would scatter like hares; and they didn't.

I ran inside; but everything had changed. The armoires, open. The saints—out of their frames, standing upright!

A little bird, completely blue, was flying, forever, in the same place, within my reach; I couldn't catch it or frighten it away.

The braid fell from my hair, the dress from my body, the white lilies fell, and the cup.

I was left hanging from I don't know what,

and from nothing.

En el claror del alba iban los familiares entre las olivas, buscando presas.

Vi hervirse papas blancas como mármol, papas grises como topos, apios, pajaritos.

En la mitad de la mañana era el primer almuerzo, y a las doce, y tres horas después.

Concurría a todos, por estricta obligación, y por gusto. A comer, detalladamente, papas grises como topos, apios, pajaritos.

El abuelo observaba mirando hacia otro lado, comía lejos.

A veces, en los intervalos, iba a visitar a algún vecino o algún amigo.

Y yo padecía su sombra de loba y rosacruz.

Al descender la tarde, cometas de otros niños cruzaban cerca. Rojas, rosadas, amarillas, eran señales.

Andábamos por los oscuros comedores,
corredores. Y algún fugaz visitante
sexual era atendido o evitado.

Y clavelinas, tenebrarios, tenebrarios, clavelinas, y más cosas.

In the clear light of dawn my relatives walked through the olive trees, hunting for prey.

I saw, boiling, white potatoes like marble, gray potatoes like moles, celery, little birds.

At midmorning came the first lunch, and then at noon, and three hours later.

I attended them all, out of compulsory duty, and out of pleasure. To eat, meticulously, gray potatoes like moles, celery, little birds.

Grandfather watched, looking the other way, eating faraway.

Sometimes, between meals, he'd visit a neighbor or a friend.

And I suffered his shadow of a she-wolf and Rosicrucian.

As the afternoon faded, other children's kites flew near. Red, pink, yellow, they were signals.

We walked through the dark kitchen doors,

corridors. And some passing visitor,

driven by lust, was admitted or evaded.

And carnations, Tenebrae candles, Tenebrae candles, carnations, and more.

Las casas campesinas guardan huesos, huevos.

En la noche de los relámpagos, desde la cama, los veía brillar.

Bajo las mesas iban perros, gatos y murciélagos; cada uno persiguiendo a su perseguidor. Por el aire había caballos pequeños como moscas; de esa colmena de caballos venía el sonido.

Se abrían todos los caminos de la vida, pero, ¿dónde poner los ojos?

Crisantemas color crema, rizadas, me rodearon toda la cama, como en un funeral.

Aventuré una mano entre ellas.

O el viento me removió los cabellos.

Y, nunca, entendí cómo se salía del altar.

The houses in the country store bones, eggs.

When lightning lit the night, from my bed, I saw them shine.

Under the tables raced dogs, cats, and bats, each in pursuit of its pursuer. In the air fluttered little horses like flies; that hive of horses was murmuring.

All the paths of life unfolding, but where to look?

Cream-colored chrysanthemums, curly, surrounded my bed, as at a funeral.

I reached in with one hand.

Or the wind ruffled my hair.

And I never knew how to step down from the altar.

Alguna mañana siento tal temor que me acuesto tratando de ocupar el menor sitio, no como casi, o sólo agua.

Me llevan a la mesa, me intervienen quirúrgicamente; de bien adentro de mí, sacan objetos monstruosos: relojes, muñecas, muchísimos dientes y peines, y huevos, huevos, huevos, azules, blancos y rosados, infinitamente, como si yo fuera una paloma de cuatro alas.

No sé si moriré.

...Y a la mitad de la tarde me apresan, otra vez.

One morning I'm so afraid that I lie down and try to take up as little space as possible, I hardly eat, or only drink water.

They carry me to the table, they operate on me; from deep inside of me, they remove monstrous objects: clocks, dolls, several teeth and combs, and eggs, eggs, eggs, blue, white, and pink eggs, endlessly, as if I were a four-winged dove.

I don't know if I'll die.

…And in the middle of the afternoon they grab me, again.

Recuerda la Primera Comunión, a los veinticinco años, y con el vestido verde que dejaba los pechos desnudos. Su madre la acompañó, escalera por escalera, hasta el altar que estaba lejísimo, cerca del cielo; y a trechos, se detenían y la madre bebía y almorzaba y proseguía acompañándola, hasta que ella tocó los pies de la Divinidad y se efectuó la Comunión.

Y el descenso, con el asustante vestido verde que dejaba afuera los pezones.

She remembers her First Communion, when she was twenty-five, and wore a green dress that exposed her bare breasts. Her mother escorted her, staircase by staircase, to the altar that was high up, close to heaven; and here and there, they stopped and her mother would drink and eat lunch and escort her onward, until she touched the feet of the Divinity and received Communion.

Then the descent, in the scary green dress that exposed her nipples.

De súbito, en la noche, misteriosamente, silenciosamente, la mariposa apareció. Se puso en un costado de la taza, venciendo graves leyes.

Traía un vestido, moderno, grande, casi sin forma, de un verde celestial, con puntos más oscuros, o plateados.

No quise llamar la atención sobre ella porque temía al otro comensal. Que arrimara un cigarrillo, pusiera fuego a esa gasa.

Temía al otro comensal, y temo a todo el mundo.

La mariposa no se iba.

Yo temblaba, levemente; el otro tuvo una actitud indefinible.

Por cortar la situación, propuse: —Vamos a bailar.

Y luego: —Vamos al jardín.

Y, de pronto, dije: —Deseo que Irma se haya ido.

Sin querer le había puesto el nombre Irma y había hablado en voz alta.

Mi acompañante respondió:

—Pero, si era un muchacho.

Disimulando, pregunté: —¿Quién?

—El de la camisa celeste, allá en tu taza.

Suddenly, at night, mysteriously, silently, the butterfly appeared. She settled on the rim of my cup, defying solemn laws.

She was wearing a large, modern dress, almost shapeless; it was a celestial green, with dark or silver dots.

I didn't want to draw attention to her since I was afraid of my companion across the table. That he might reach out with his cigarette and light that gauze on fire.

I was afraid of my companion, and I'm afraid of the whole world.

The butterfly wouldn't go away.

I trembled a little; my partner wore an inscrutable expression.

To escape from the situation, I suggested, "Let's dance."

And then, "Let's go to the garden."

And suddenly I said, "I wish Irma had gone away."

Without realizing it, I had named her Irma and spoken out loud.

My companion replied:

"But he was a boy."

Acting naturally, I asked, "Who?"

"In the sky-blue shirt, there on your cup."

Puse un huevo, blanco, puro, brillante; parecía una estrella ovalada. Ya, con intervalo de años, había dado otro, celeste, y otro, de color de rosa; pero, éste era puro, blanco, brillante, y el más bello. Lo coloqué en una taza, con una mano arriba, para que no se le fuera el brillo; lo mimé con discreción, con cierta fingida indiferencia. Las mujeres quedaron envidiosas, insidiosas; me criticaban; ostensivamente, se cubrían los hombros, y se alargaron los vestidos.

Proseguí, impertérrita.

No puedo decir qué salió del huevo porque no lo sé; pero, sea lo que sea, aún me sigue; su sombra, filial y dulce, se abate sobre mí.

I laid an egg, white, spotless, shiny; it looked like an oval star. Already, years apart, I had produced another, sky blue, and another, pink; but this one was spotless, white, shiny, the most beautiful. I placed it in a cup, my hand held over it, so it wouldn't lose its glow; I fussed over it discreetly, with a certain feigned indifference. The women grew envious, insidious; they criticized me; ceremoniously, they covered their shoulders and smoothed their dresses.

I carried on, undaunted.

I can't say what hatched from the egg since I don't know; but, whatever it was, it still follows me; its shadow, filial, gentle, descends on me.

Caía una lluvia finísima, que no mojaba, casi. Atamos las muñecas en las ramas, como castigo, las que se habían portado mal. Con un rumor de animalillos se levantaban los hongos de cabeza parda, semejantes a osos; en pocos minutos quedaron más altos que nosotras. Y algo más subía de la tierra, rotas copas, candeleros, de antiguos festivales, que presuponíamos, vagamente.

Y la luna celeste, color limón, andaba con la lluvia. Hasta que vino mamá y la tocó. Y cortaba pimpollos, desató las muñecas; yendo hacia la casa dio un breve grito. Acudimos, puntuales. Y desaparecimos, en su falda, en su vientre.

Y todo quedó en paz.

A faint rain was falling, hardly dampening anything. We tied the dolls to the branches, to punish them, the ones who had misbehaved. Squealing like little animals, the brown-capped mushrooms were sprouting, resembling bears; after a few minutes they were taller than we were. And something else rose from the earth, broken chalices, candlesticks, from ancient ceremonies, of which we had an inkling.

And the moon, blue, lemon-colored, came out with the rain. Until mama came and touched it. And she cut flowers, untied the dolls; on her way to the house she shouted. We came to her, quickly. And disappeared into her lap, her belly.

And all was quiet.

Los animales hablaban; las vacas y caballos de mi padre, sus aves, sus ovejas. Largos raciocinios, parlamentos; discusiones entre sí y con los hombres, en procura de las frutas, de los hongos, de la sal. Yo iba por el bosque y veía al sol bajar, a la vez, en varios lugares; cuatro o cinco soles, redondos, blancos como nieve, de largos hilos. O cuadrados y rojos, de largos hilos. Mi padre era el príncipe de los prados. Pero, algunas mañanas lo desconocía, aunque a toda hora soñaba con él. Y, también, olvidé mi nombre (Rosa), y me iba por los prados, y, entonces, nadie se atrevió a llamarme. Y yo pasaba, lejos, de sombrero azul, envuelta en llamas.

The animals spoke; my father's cows and horses, his birds, his sheep. Well-reasoned arguments, oratories; deliberations with each other and with the men, in pursuit of fruit, mushrooms, salt. I would walk through the forest and see the sun set in several places, simultaneously; four or five suns, round, white as snow, with long threads. Or square and red, with long threads. My father was the prince of the pastures. But some mornings I didn't recognize him, although I dreamed of him continuously. And I forgot my name (Rosa), and I wandered the pastures, and then no one dared call to me. And I walked, in the distance, in a blue hat, wrapped in flames.

Mariposas celestes, grandes, fuertes, consistentes, casi de raso, con las puntas labradas, tal si las hubiera hecho una modista y bordadora, modista y mariposa.

Y otra, amarilla, única, que apareció un día, refulgente igual que el oro, callada como el oro; sobre la que se abalanzaron todos los habitantes de la casa, porque era amarilla y sola, sin saber a qué. Mariposas negras en banda, subieron de lo hondo, cuando mamá tenía cinco años y acertó a pasar en carruaje. Y nunca pudo olvidar aquello.

Mariposa celeste mía, cazada una mañana de abril entre los nardos; vino a estar en un libro; la miré a través de mucho tiempo y en los días de enfermedad. Mártir de hojas celestes; talle de uva, de lágrima negra.

Mariposa color de fuego cruzó entre las otras como el ángel de los exterminios, clavel con señas; alcancé a verle el rostro bajo la capota punzó.

Mariposa blanca del día de las muertas. Lejos del féretro y las lágrimas. Crece sobre el ropero, los objetos de tocador, como una espuma, un encaje.

La topamos sin saber qué es.

Mi disfraz de mariposa; grandes alones con manchas. Papá los construyó, trabajosamente.

Y con él, de niña, enfrenté al mundo,

los zorros y los pájaros.

Sky-blue butterflies, large, strong, sturdy, like satin, embroidered at the tips, as if a seamstress had sewn them by hand, butterfly and bodkin.

And another, yellow, all by itself, that appeared one day, shining like gold, quiet as gold; everyone in the house, without thinking, leaping after it, since it was yellow and different. Swarms of black butterflies, which rose from the depths, when mama was five and happened to pass by in a carriage. And she never could forget.

My blue butterfly, caught one April morning by the spikenards; it ended up inside a book; I looked at it years later and on days when I was sick. Martyr of blue leaves; its body like a grape, a black tear.

Fiery red butterfly that fluttered with the others, angel of exterminations, carnation that emits signals; I made out its face under a scarlet bonnet.

White butterfly on the day of the dead. Far from the casket and tears. It spreads across the armoire, the items on the vanity, like froth, lace.

We brush into it without knowing what it is.

My butterfly costume; wide spotted wings. Papa labored over them.

And wearing it, as a child, I faced the world,
the foxes and finches.

Había marimonias por todas partes. Azules, rojas, rosadas, amarillas, color leche. Sobre todo, rojas, rosadas, amarillas, negro el centro, la corona de fuego. Como rostros, estrellas de la tierra.

En ese estío, yo, que era de tan breve edad, crecí varios años, y entendía todo como si fuera mayor. Y los cazadores trajeron liebres para mamá, zorros, mariposas rarísimas, una negra, con un brillante en cada punta, que se nos huyó al jardín, y hasta dijo una canción.

Y en un atardecer ocurrió algo insólito, creo que el nacimiento de mi hermana.

Había muchas luces; en los estantes resplandecían las ciruelas, y la estrella de los magos se detuvo.

There were Persian buttercups everywhere. Blue, red, pink, yellow, the color of milk. Especially red, pink, and yellow, dark at the center, wreathed with fire. Like faces, terrestrial stars.

That summer, when I was only a child, I aged several years, and understood everything as if I were older. And the hunters brought hares for my mother, foxes, rare butterflies, a black one with diamond-tipped wings, which escaped to the garden, and even let out a song.

And early one evening something unusual happened, I think it was when my sister was born.

There were many lights; on the shelves glittered plums, and the star of the Magi hovered.

Vamos por la pared.

Mamá tiene alas marrones, sedosas; yo, alas violetas; al entreabrirlas se les ve varias capas de gasa. Proseguimos por el muro; con antenas finísimas tocando ramitas, ramas, de bálsamo, de perejil, y otras cosas.

Parece que estamos libres de los semejantes que son azogue.

La luna es, a cada minuto, más blanca y oscura.

Y resplandece por todo el prado, aquí, allá, la Virgen de los insectos.

Con ala y diadema y muchísimos pies.

We fly along the wall.

Mama's wings are brown, silk; mine, violet; when they spread open, layers of gauze unfold. We follow the wall; our thin antennae grazing branches, boughs, of balsam, parsley, and other things.

It seems we've broken away from our quicksilver peers.

The moon is, with each minute, whiter and darker.

And throughout the meadow shines, here, there, the Virgin of insects.

With wing and diadem and many feet.

Los oscuros nísperos extienden oleadas de aroma a vino, a azúcar.

Siempre, con mi viejo traje, me senté en una peña. El cielo echaba los últimos resplandores. La compañía de Teatro de los Huertos terminó los ensayos y se disipó un poco. Una mesa serviría de escena. Avizoré el paisaje. Los ánades ponen muchísimos huevos. El mismo pájaro da huevos de diversos colores. Rojos, azules, con manchas, como pintados al óleo. Por todas partes aparecen nidadas, montículos de huevos.

No sé cuál va a ser el destino de la "troupe" que ahora dirijo; todos son mayores que yo y mi reinado parece frágil.

A poco, comienzan a presentarse habitantes de todas las huertas, y se sientan en el suelo mirando hacia el escenario.

Así, la actuación estuvo, otra vez; pero, los violeros, a ratos, languidecían, y eran sustituidos por integrantes del público, y la línea entre la realidad y el sueño, se desdibuja.

La noche devoró, totalmente, al jardín de nísperos.

Y las ánades en sus ocultos sitiales, preparan más huevos rojos.

The dark loquats waft whiffs of wine, of sugar.

As usual, in my old dress, I sat on a rock. The sky was launching its final bursts. The cast of the Theater of the Orchards stopped rehearsing and started to scatter. A table would serve as the stage. I surveyed the landscape. The mallards are laying many eggs. The same bird produces eggs of different colors. Red, blue, speckled, as if painted in oils. All over appear clutches, mounds of eggs.

I don't know what'll happen to the "troupe" I'm currently directing; they're all older than me and my tenure seems fragile.

Little by little, the people who live throughout the orchards start showing up, and they sit in the grass, staring at the stage.

So, the performance took place again; but the viola players, now and then, faded, and members of the audience filled in for them, and the line between dreams and reality blurred.

The night consumed the entire loquat garden.

And the mallards, hidden in their seats of honor, fashion more red eggs.

Dejo la casa donde camas y roperos están sembrados, tienen raíces; sus patas echan hojas, rosas. Los familiares, en la cocina, hablan, hacen larguísimos comentarios.

Cruzo el jardín y los jardines que están más allá del jardín.

Veo árboles al azar. Y zapallos, chatos y dorados. Me siento sobre uno. Desde las tres de la tarde, hay estrellas, y, ahora, que va a caer la tarde, el cielo se torna deslumbrador; los caballos dejan de beber y miran con un poco de asombro a esas diademas. Continúo, las flores son clavelinas, celedonias, clavelinas, y su perfume a miel, a azúcar, a clavel.

A ratos, un golpe de viento sacude los jardines.

Y caen algunas estrellas blancas y menudas como arroz; tiendo la mano y devoro, y prosigo; sin prisa, de prisa; sin rumbo; a veces, me detengo y retrocedo; pero, es inútil, porque las flores se cierran para siempre, tras de mí.

I leave the house, where the beds and armoires have been sown, rooted; their legs sprout leaves, roses. In the kitchen my family is talking, chatting endlessly.

I cross the garden and the gardens beyond the garden.

I see trees here and there. And gourds, squat and gold. I sit on one of them. At three in the afternoon, the stars came out, and now, as the afternoon fades, the sky is dazzling; the horses stop drinking and look up, a bit astonished by those diadems. I keep walking, the flowers are pinks, celandines, pinks, and their fragrance of honey, sugar, carnations.

Now and then, a gust of wind whips through the garden.

And a few white stars fall, tiny as rice; I hold out my hand and devour, and I keep going; unhurried, in a hurry; aimlessly; sometimes, I stop and go back; but it's useless, since the flowers close forever, behind me.

Verdes, color rosa, anilladas, dibujadas. Se dice de ellas que tienen relaciones consigo, y se las ve en el espasmo.

O rígidas como un dedo alcanzan a beber en la fuente de las rosas. Están emparentadas con las rosas, las romelias y el peral. Las consideran sólo ensueños, representación de los pecados de los hombres.

Pero, yo, de niñita, a la luz del sol y de la luna, creo en ellas, sé que son, de verdad.

Las vi abrir los labios, negros como la noche, la dentadura de oro, en pos de una almendra, una pepita de calabaza;

enfrentar la propia línea, jugando y peleando; y en el amor a solas, retorcerse hasta morir.

Green, pink, ringed, hand-drawn. It's said they have relations with themselves, and are visible when they shudder.

Or rigid like a finger they manage to drink from the fountain of roses. They're related to roses, bromeliads, and the pear tree. Some consider them only reveries that represent the sins of men.

But I, as a girl, in the light of the sun and moon, believe in them; I know they're real.

I saw them open their lips, black as the night, their gold teeth, after an almond, a pumpkin seed.

to face one's own mark, playing and fighting; and in love without others, to twist until death.

El caracol, esa espiral de humo que no crece, con el borde intensamente rosado, un querube, un quéramos exquisito. De pronto, saca la frente y los pies transparentes, y camina como un señor, una señorita de los cielos, de los fúnebres, tiene sordas bocinas sexuales. Es, a la vez, el señor y la señorita. En ese pedacito blanco están Hermes y Afrodita; así, se detiene y se conjuga, solo. Y, luego, del segundo perturbador, prosigue, sobre las caras rosadas de las rosas, como una carroza, una miniporcelana trashumante.

Hasta que dejo de mirar.

O cae al pasto esa cajita, redonda, desolada.

The snail, that whorl of smoke that never rises, with a radiant pink rim, a cherub, a cherishment. Suddenly, it pokes out its forehead and invisible feet, and walks like a man, a maiden of the heavens, of the dirges, its carnal trumpets are never heard. It is, simultaneously, man and maiden. In that white shard dwell Hermes and Aphrodite; just like that, it stops and mates with itself. And after an agonizing second, it continues, across the pink facades of the roses, like a carriage, a wandering porcelain figurine.

Until I stop watching.

Or that little box, round, empty, falls in the grass.

Dijo "Mariposa" "Amelia". Y me volví en el aire oscuro de la tarde de oro. Entre los higos como flores cerradas, pesadas y violetas.

Dijo "Amelia", un antiguo nombre, tal vez, el mío, el verdadero, antes de nacer.

Era el Dios que hablaba, era el Puma.

Me volví,

buscando su cara de oro, su invisible huella.

Mas, nada había; sólo el viento que jugaba, como siempre, en el jardín de higos y violetas.

A voice said, "Butterfly," "Amelia." And I spun around in the dark air on a golden afternoon. Between the figs, like flower buds, heavy and violet.

A voice said, "Amelia," an ancient name, perhaps mine, my true name, before birth.

It was God who spoke; it was the Puma.

I spun around,

searching for his gold face, his invisible trace.

But nothing was there; only the wind playing, as always, in the garden of figs and violets.

Había nacido con zapatos. Rojos, finos, de taco alto, que fueron la desesperación de todos los que vivimos juntos en aquel tiempo.

Y en la cara tenía varias dentaduras, y lentes celestes como el fuego.

Al pasar, por la tarde, parecía el ángel de la devoración con pie punzó.

Mas, en realidad, amó la luz solar. Comía guindas, llevándose una a cada boca.

Y sentía temor y amor hacia el Maestro Tigre que llegaba en la noche a buscar doncellas.

Y nunca la eligió.

She was born with shoes. Red, elegant, with high heels, which were the desperation of all of us who lived together at that time.

And on her face she had several sets of teeth, and glasses, light blue as fire.

Strolling in the afternoon, she looked like the angel of voracity with scarlet feet.

But actually she loved the sunlight. She ate cherries, lifting one to each mouth.

And she felt fear and love towards the Master Tiger who came at night in search of maidens.

And never chose her.

Dónde apareció la Virgen? Si pensamos, en un ramo de jazmín, en el frasco con azúcar, en el desván, la sala, la cocina, en el jardín. Estaba por todos lados. A la vez, por todos lados. Con el vestido blanco, y capuchón, y en la mano, no sé qué, una fresia o un pollito. Yo quedé harta de esa repetición, reverberación. No era que me mirase; ella miraba hacia abajo, hacia adelante. Llamé a alguien que ni estaba, para que cortara eso. A ratos, todo quedó vacío, claro, no dormía, sonreía; pero, en el sueño, ella sacaba, otra vez, un ala. Y de ahí a la realidad. La otra ala, las plumas; y en la mano no sé qué, un pollito o una fresia.

Los volados de cristal.

Where did the Virgin appear? If we think about it, in a jasmine bouquet, in the sugar jar, in the attic, the living room, the kitchen, in the garden. She was everywhere. Everywhere all at once. In her white dress, and mantle, and something, a freesia or baby chick, in her hand. I grew tired of that repetition, reverberation. She didn't look at me; she looked at the ground, or straight ahead. I called to someone who wasn't even there, to break it off. Now and then, everything went empty, clear; I awoke, smiling; but, in the dream, she extended again a wing. And from there into reality. The other wing, her feathers; and something, a baby chick or freesia, in her hand.

Her glass ruffles.

Bajó una mariposa a un lugar oscuro; al parecer, de hermosos colores; no se distinguía bien. La niña más chica creyó que era una muñeca rarísima y la pidió; los otros niños dijeron: —Bajo las alas hay un hombre.

Yo dije: —Sí, su cuerpo parece un hombrecito.

Pero, ellos aclararon que era un hombre de tamaño natural. Me arrodillé y vi. Era verdad lo que decían los niños. ¿Cómo cabía un hombre de tamaño normal bajo las alitas?

Llamamos a un vecino. Trajo una pinza. Sacó las alas. Y un hombre alto se irguió y se marchó.

Y esto que parece casi increíble, luego, fue pintado prodigiosamente en una caja.

A butterfly descended to a dark spot; it seemed to have lovely colors; it was hard to tell. The youngest of the girls thought it was a rare doll and wanted it for herself; the other children said, "Beneath the wings there's a man."

I said, "Yes, its body looks like a little man."

But they explained it was a full-sized man. I knelt down and saw. What the children said was true. How could a normal-sized man fit beneath those tiny wings?

We called over a neighbor. He brought tweezers, removed the wings. A tall man stood and walked off.

And all this, which seems almost incredible, later inexplicably was painted on a box.

Mi padre y mi madre me cercaban. Si iba hacia el norte estaba mi padre; si iba hacia el sur, también, estaba.

Si iba hacia el este, estaba mamá; y en el oeste, también estaba.

Y ambos estaban en las cuatro partes.

No sé cómo pude llegar a la escuela y al altar, cruzar los jardines.

Creo que era sonámbula y en sueños me escapaba; me iba desnuda; pero, al volverme, aún en el sueño, venía mama; y me daba miedo, me daba vergüenza.

...Me parece que, hoy, es el día de mi nacimiento. Papá y mamá dicen "Se llamará Marosa".

Y grita el viento.

Y salen tímidas violetas mártires de entre las cosas.

My mother and father surrounded me. If I headed north my father was there; if I headed south he was still there.

If I headed east, mama was there; and in the west, still she was there.

And both of them were on all four sides.

I don't know how I made it to school and the altar, how I crossed the gardens.

I think I was sleepwalking and in my dreams I escaped; and I walked naked; but when I returned, still in the dream, mama would come; and I was afraid, and ashamed.

…I think that today is the day that I am born. Mama and papa say, "She'll be called Marosa."

And the wind howls.

And out from under things sprout shy, martyred violets.

Soy la Virgen. Me doy cuenta. En la noche me paro junto a las columnas y a las fuentes. O salgo a la carretera, donde los conductores me miran extasiados o huyen como locos.

Soy la Virgen. El Ángel me hablaba entre jazmines y en varios planos. Me dijo algo rarísimo; no entendí bien.

Voy por el antiguo huerto —Isabel, Ana— por las antiguas casas; quisiera ser una mujer en una de estas casas, una mujer en la ciudad, pero, soy la Virgen; no se dan cuenta; busco otra aldea abandonada, otros cáñamos. Silba el viento. Los lobos están comiendo los corderos. A mi diadema caen las estrellas como lágrimas, caen rosas y gladiolos, dalias negras.

Soy la Virgen.

Estoy sola. Silba el viento. ¿Adónde voy? ¿Adónde voy?

Y jamás habrá respuesta.

I'm the Virgin. I realize. At night I stand by the pillars and fountains. Or I go to the road, where the drivers stare at me, mesmerized, or flee frantically.

I'm the Virgin. The Angel would speak to me among jasmine and on several levels. He said a strange thing; I didn't understand.

I wander through the old orchard—Isabel, Ana—through the old houses; I'd like to be a woman in one of these houses, a city woman, but I'm the Virgin; they don't realize; I search for another deserted village, other fields of hemp. The wind whistles. The wolves are eating the lambs. On my diadem fall stars like tears, fall roses and gladioli, black dahlias.

I'm the Virgin.

I'm alone. The wind whistles. Where to go? Where to go?

And there's never an answer.

Rosana, Rosana y Rosana volvían del baile. En el aire oscuro de la noche, de antes del alba. El pelo suelto, las enaguas de raso hasta el suelo. Cayeron unas agujas, largas como espinas de grandes pescados. El contorno de las peras era brillante. Parecían docenas de dibujos colgantes de las ramas. Un pájaro gritó como si no estuviese acostumbrado a la enorme soledad. Una oveja se levantó y se fue. Los trabajadores nocturnos seguían ordeñando leche, aceite y licor de las perennes vacas.

Las tres Rosanas llegaron a la casa. Soltaron sus rizos, (las peinetas con coral en las esquinas) las enaguas, reñían por los novios. Se durmieron con la cándida mano en la almohada.

Y en el corazón de los aparadores, las tacitas volaban quietas. Como vuelan los ángeles. Y una rata puso un huevo, blanco, almendrado, celeste. Que nadie vio.

Rosana, Rosana, and Rosana were coming home from the dance. In the dark night air, before the dawn. Their hair down, their satin petticoats touching the ground. A few pins fell, long as the bones of fish. The outline of the pears glistened. They resembled dozens of drawings hanging from the branches. A bird cried out as if unaccustomed to the enormous solitude. A sheep stood up and wandered off. The graveyard shift continued drawing milk, oil, and alcohol from the perennial cows.

The three Rosanas arrived at the house. They loosened their curls, (the combs with coral at the corners) their petticoats; they quarreled over boys. Each slept with a pristine hand on the pillow.

And in the heart of the sideboards, the teacups flew without fluttering. The way angels fly. And a rat laid an egg, white, almond, sky blue. That nobody saw.

El día de mi nacimiento estaban todos los frutos. Las manzanas, rojas y picudas como estrellas, peras de alabastro, cruzadas por jazmines, nísperos en forma de joyas, anillos o pendientes (pero, se les reconocía por el aroma), tandas de lirios y claveles, uvas y rosas en todos los colores. Y los ánades en el patio, lagartijas, moscas, liebres, lobizones. Toda la Creación estaba allí, esperando con ansiedad a aquel ser nuevo que venía. Y yo me despegué desde lo más hondo de mi madre, me erguí con el cabello rojo que se iba por el suelo, y mi extraña identidad.

On the day I was born all the fruits were there. The apples, red and pointed like stars, alabaster pears, crossed with jasmine, loquats in the shape of jewels, rings or earrings (but you could tell them apart by the scent), waves of lilies and carnations, grapes and roses in each and every color. And mallard ducks on the patio, little lizards, flies, hares, werewolves. All of Creation was there, anxiously awaiting the new creature on its way. And I pulled myself from the depths of my mother, I stood upright with red hair that flowed to the ground, and my strange identity.

Ser liebre.

Le veo las orejas como hojas, los ojos pardos, los bigotes de pistilo, un tic en la boca oscura, de alhelí.

Va, paso a paso, por las galerías abandonadas del campo.

Se mueve con un rumor de tambor. ¿Será un jefe liebre? ¿una liebre madre? ¿O un hombre liebre? ¿una mujer liebre? ¿Seré yo misma? Me toco las orejas delicadas, los ojos pardos, el bigote fino, la boca de alhelí, la dentadura anacarada, oscura.

Cerca, lejos, pían las liebres pollas.

Viene un olor de trébol, de margaritas amarillas de todo el campo, viene un olor de trébol.

Y las viejas estrellas se mueven como hojas.

To be a hare.

I see its ears like leaves, its brown eyes, its whiskers like pistils, a twitching in the mouth, the dark center of a stock flower.

It goes, step by step, through the empty corridors of the fields.

It moves to the sound of a faint drum. Is it a head hare? a mother hare? Or a hare man? a hare woman? Is it me? I touch my soft ears, brown eyes, thin whiskers, my stock-flower mouth, my dark and pearly teeth.

Nearby, faraway, the chicken hares chirp.

A scent of clover fills the air, of yellow daisies from all the fields, a scent of clover in the air.

And the ancient stars sway like leaves.

Tenía la falda cargada de rosas; en las faldas le nacían rosas. Quería disimular; se empolvaba el rostro, tejía sus trenzas, comía a la luz del sol, para parecer como las otras. Mas, de su falda brotaban rosas. Fue a consultar al cura y al juez; que nada pudieron; acudió a los animales: liras, hurones, lobizones; miraron un poco y se fueron; una vaca intentó comer las flores y desistió.

Volvió a la casa; la madre cocía hongos, en varias sartenes, y les echaba fresias, y alguna hierba levemente maligna, para que quedara más enigmático el manjar.

Ella entró con su falda cargada de rosas, florida de rosas; la madre cerró la puerta con fuerza, para que no llegaran, también, picaflores y mariposas.

Ella se sentó, quedamente, y comía su pan.

Her skirt was full of roses; in her lap roses were blooming. She tried to act naturally; she'd powder her face, braid her hair, and eat in the sunlight, like the other girls. But roses sprouted from her skirt. She went to consult the priest and judge; who could do nothing; she turned to the animals: lyrebirds, ferrets, werewolves; they glanced at her and left; a cow tried to eat the flowers and gave up.

She went back home; her mother was cooking mushrooms in several pans, sprinkling them with freesias and a mildly malignant herb to make the dish more enigmatic.

She entered with her skirt full of roses, flowering with roses; her mother slammed the door shut, to keep out the hummingbirds and butterflies.

She sat down quietly and ate her bread.

de Mesa de esmeralda

from Emerald Tablet

(1985)

Las cabras monteses vuelan de nube en nube, de parva en parva, de casa en casa. Los cuernos, largos y curvos, más largos que ellas, parecen tocar el suelo.

Si cruzan por las nubes caen trizadas las madreselvas; si cruzan por la tierra ni se estremecen las madreselvas.

Hay tiempos en que comen todo; no resta ninguna cosa en las paredes y el subsuelo. Sus ojos chispean; se encienden y apagan. Y dan hijas que pueden ser palomas o vaquitas, (nunca crecen y quedan abandonadas en la yerba, y dan miedo a los humanos).

Pero todo esto estuvo muy bien escrito en el libro primero de la escuela, en el segundo y en los otros. Y lo enseñaron en el liceo, y lo representé en el Teatro. Hice de cabra; y de su hija, que era distinta, tenía pétalos.

The mountain goats fly from cloud to cloud, haystack to haystack, house to house. Their horns, long and curved, longer than them, seem to touch the ground.

If they race across the clouds the honeysuckle falls in shreds; if they race across the earth the honeysuckle doesn't even quiver.

Sometimes they eat everything; nothing is left on the walls and in the subsoil. Their eyes flicker; they blaze and extinguish. And they have daughters, who might be doves or calves, (they never grow and are left in the grass, and they frighten the humans).

But this was all written down in the first schoolbook, and the second, and in the others. And it was taught in the high school, and I performed it in the Theater. I played the mountain goat; and her daughter, who was different, who had petals.

Una noche mala, de lluvia y nieve, entró un querube a casa; mamá le destinó un lugar subalterno, entre almohadones, cerca de los perros, gatos y muñecas. Papá le llamó "la lámpara", lo tomó por una cosa; la hermana y prima, más pequeñas, creyéronlo un juguete y jugaban con él; mas, la prima huyó diciendo: —El bicho me quemó.

Su relumbre era exquisito, denunciador de jerarquía.

Me mantuve aparte, tensa, y entreabría la puerta para que volviera a su origen.

Él no hizo caso, y permaneció por semanas. Iba de pared en pared. Y cambiaba. Negro, grande, con formato de mosca, flotaba sobre el agua de floreros y de fuentes.

Pareció copular con algunos objetos.

Hasta que puso un huevo sombrío, brillante y vacío.

On a dreary night of rain and snow, a cherub entered the house; mama allotted it a lowly spot, on cushions, by the dogs, cats, and dolls. Papa called it "the lamp," mistook it for a device; my sister and cousin, who were younger, thought it was a toy and played with it; but my cousin ran away, saying: "The bug burned my hand."

Its radiance was exquisite, unveiling hierarchies.

I kept my distance, uneasy, and left the door cracked open so it would go back where it came from.

It ignored me, and stayed for weeks. It would travel from wall to wall. And transform. Large, black, in the shape of a fly, it hovered over the water in vases and fountains.

It seemed to copulate with some of the objects.

Until it laid an egg, somber, bright, and empty.

El jabalí venía desde la lejana selva a robar naranjas. Las cerdas, en su corral, quedaban como locas, en celo, entreabrían la cabeza rosada.

Pero él parecía querer naranjas. Mas, luego, iba por ellas, a acuciarles y poseerles con furia loca.

Mi padre salía gritando con palos y con balas, y nombres extraordinarios: "¡Ya volvió Ese! ¡Ahí está don Pablo!".

Para mí, el jabalí era un hombre y jabalí. Rogué por él. Que nunca le alcanzasen! Y él, siempre fugó con su oscuro trote al lejano punto de donde era venido.

Una noche, mi padre desconfió algo, y entró de súbito en mi habitación, prendió la lámpara. Yo estaba como dormida, el pelo suelto, las manos juntas. En el estante, la Virgen, y debajo, jazmines, y huevos de paloma y de gallina, sobre cada uno de los cuales, yo había pintado un jabalí con impresionante cuerno y pies inalcanzables.

The boar would come from the distant forest to steal oranges. In their pen, the sows in heat went wild, their pink heads starting to poke out.

But he seemed to want oranges. Then, later, he went after the sows, to rouse and possess them with mad fury.

My father would run outside shouting with sticks and bullets, and extraordinary names: "Back again, that One! If it isn't don Pablo!"

In my mind, the boar was a man and a boar. I prayed for him. That he would elude them again! And he, always escaped at a dark gallop to the distant point where he was come.

One night, my father suspected something, and entered my room abruptly, lit the lamp. I stayed still, as if asleep, my hair down, my hands clasped. On the shelf, the Virgin, and below, jasmine, and hen and dove eggs, on each of which I had painted a boar with a formidable horn and elusive feet.

Mamá, tu corazón que late y late, tus margaritas apostólicas, romanas, tu delantal marrón con nudos, donde, cuando estás sentada, se sienta el diablo. El diablo parece un perro pequeño con los ojos bajos. Pero, si lo miro mucho entreabre las pupilas verdes como tizones y me mira tal si fuera a devorarme o a devorar el mundo. Entonces, yo huyo al jardín, o me siento junto al ropero y continúo la puntilla que iniciamos cuando nací, las carpetas amarillas, el mantel eterno, el hilado. Y al caer la tarde las arañas huyen a dormir en el centro de su red. Y bajo el techo cuelga una estrella parda.

Te digo: —Mamá, ata el diablo fuera, átale al diamelo, que cuide el jardín.

Pero nos da pena y hasta le traemos almohadones y un tazón de leche.

El aire, fuera, es finísimo, brillante; caen perlas muy blancas y piedras azules.

Lejos, hay un rumor de bailes; en los más lejanos horizontes hay un rumor de baile y de pelea.

Mama, your heart that beats and beats, your daises, Roman, Catholic, your knotted brown apron, where, when you're sitting, the devil sits. The devil looks like a little dog with downcast eyes. But if I watch him long enough his pupils widen, green as embers, and he looks at me as if he were going to devour me or devour the whole world. So I escape to the garden, or I sit by the armoire and continue the lace we began when I was born, the yellow doilies, the eternal tablecloth, the spinning. And at dusk the spiders hurry back to the center of their web to sleep. And under the roof hangs a brown star.

I say, "Mama, tie up the devil outside, tie him to the jasmine, so he'll look after the garden."

But we feel sorry for him and even bring him cushions and a bowl of milk.

The air outside is very fine, shimmering; white pearls and blue pebbles are falling.

From a distance comes the sound of dancing; from the furthest horizons comes the sound of dancing and fighting.

Mi oficio: rezadora.

Mamá me sacó de adentro de un manzano. De arriba de una manzana redonda y blanca que pendía de una rama. Yo era oscura, tornasol. Y levantaba la pata hacia Dios. Y mamá dijo: –Ven aquí, recitadora. Y me tomó como hija, me llevó a casa, me entregó a papá, las tías, a la hermana y a las primas, que, al mirarme de reojo, me quisieron, y hasta enclavaron un pequeño teatro en mitad de la cocina, del comedor y de la mesa, para que prosiguiese mis murmurio y oración. Y yo representaba a la caída de la tarde, entre retamas, en el silencio, o sobre el almohadón de gatos.

Hoy, en mi frágil cabeza hay un brillante. Papá ya no está.

La prima se fue lejos.

Mi hermana tiene una hija.

Mamá me mira.

Y yo,

rezo.

My labor: prayer.

Mama took me from inside an apple tree. From the top of a round white apple hanging from a branch. I was dark, iridescent. And would lift my foreleg towards God. And mama said, "Come here, recitress." And she took me in like a daughter, she carried me home, handed me to papa, the aunts, to my sister and cousins, who, out of the corners of their eyes, embraced me, and even set a little theater in the middle of the kitchen, of the dining room, and the table, so that I might continue my murmurs and prayers. And I'd perform at twilight, among broom flowers, in the silence, or on the cushion for the cats.

Today, in my fragile skull there's a jewel. Papa is gone.

My cousin moved faraway.

My sister has a daughter.

Mama looks at me.

And I,

pray.

Volvieron las vacas. Los santos se iban de las puertas con ramos de almendro y retama; no era que caminasen; el viento los llevó poniéndolos aquí o allá; sus vestidos en rojo oscuro y azules. El lucero estaba tan cerca que parecía de vidrio, un botellón.

Una voz en lo hondo de los aposentos, dijo: —Invita a los santos. Sírveles.

Corrí al umbral. Clamé: —"¡Estefanía! ¡Ratón! ¡María Inés!"

Mamá salió de detrás de las alacenas, diciendo:

—Ésos no son los nombres de los santos. Voy a poner la olla, a hacer la sopa.

Puso la olla, el agua, ramos de yuyos. Dijo: —Cázame una mariposa.

Sólo porque lo deseé, una mariposa apareció al instante.

La agarré de las alas, trémula. Era grande, negra, de cabeza blanca. Mamá la echó; se asó enseguida y quedó íntegra. Las alas abiertas sobre la sopa.

Mamá decía: —Le dará sabor y suerte.

Me azoré. Vi los años venideros. Y los del pasado. Mamá que me obligaba a cazar mariposas. El destino que las ponía en mi mano.

The cows returned. The saints were leaving through the doors with bouquets of almond blossoms and broom flowers; they didn't even walk; the wind took them, placing them here or there; their dresses dark red and blue. The evening star was so close it seemed to be made of glass, an enormous bottle.

A voice from deep within the rooms said, "Invite the saints inside. Serve them."

I ran to the doorway. And shouted, "Estefania! Mouse! Maria Ines!"

Mama emerged from behind the cupboards, saying:

"Those are not the names of the saints. I'm going to put a pot on the stove, and make soup."

She heated the pot, water, sprigs of herbs. She said, "Catch me a butterfly."

Only because I wished it so, a butterfly appeared that instant.

I snatched it by the wings, quivering. It was large, black, its head white. Mama tossed it in; it boiled instantly and remained whole. The wings spread over the soup.

Mama said, "It'll give it flavor and good luck."

I was unnerved. I saw the years to come. And those in the past. Mama, who forced me to catch butterflies. Destiny, which placed them in my hand.

Los leones rondaban la casa.

Los leones siempre rondaron.

Siempre se dijo que los leones rondaron siempre.

Parecían salir de los paraísos y el rosal.

Los leones eran sucios y dorados.

Ellos eran muy bellos.

Los ojos como perlas. Y un broche brillante en el pecho entre aquel pelo áureo.

Los leones entraron a la casa.

Corrimos a esconder los floreros de sal, de azúcar, el cometa Halley, las queridísimas sábanas nevadas, la colección de estampillas. Y a traer los sudarios.

Los leones eran al mismo tiempo, presentes e invisibles, al mismo tiempo, visibles e invisibles.

Se oía el rumor de la leche que robaban, el clamor de la miel y la carne que cortaban.

Llevaron hacia afuera a la abuela oscura, la que tenía una guía de rositas alrededor del corazón.

Y la comieron fríamente. Como en un simulacro.

Y, –¡como si hubiese sido un simulacro!– ella tornó a la casa y dijo: –Los leones rondaron siempre. Están delante de los paraísos y el rosal. Dijo: –Los leones ya están acá.

The lions would circle the house.

The lions always circled.

It always was said that the lions circled it all.

They seemed to issue from the paradises and the rosebush.

The lions were dirty and gold.

They were beautiful.

Their eyes like pearls. And on the chest a bright brooch among the gilded hair.

The lions entered the house.

We scrambled to hide the salt and sugar vases, Halley's Comet, our precious snow-white sheets, the stamp collection. And cover them with shrouds.

The lions were at the same time present and invisible, at the same time, visible and invisible.

We'd hear the slosh of the milk they stole, the cries of the honey and the meat they sliced.

They dragged away the dark grandmother, who had a garland of little roses around her heart.

And they ate her coldly. As if it were make-believe.

And (as if it had been make-believe!) she came back to the house and said, "The lions always circled. They're in front of the paradises and rosebush." She said, "The lions are here."

de La Falena

from The Moth

(1987)

Qué noche extraña cuando murió el abuelo. Caían gotas, piedras blancas, de los limones y el rosal. Desde el aparador salían ratas; las tacitas en docena, siempre doce, las copitas; los licores de todos los colores, quedaron negros.

La tía Joseph dio un grito cerca del cadáver. Nosotras, las niñas, también gritábamos. De improviso, aparecieron tías más remotas, primas de primas, súbitamente, en un minuto, como si hubiesen viajado a caballo o en mariposa. Y vecinos de las más lejanas chacras, y hasta de las chacras de subtierra, vinieron en sus carros fúnebres, cargados de sandías.

Vi alguien, rarísimo, adentro del espejo; me fijé bien por si era un reflejo; pero no había nadie que correspondiera a él.

Mas, al amanecer, los extraños partieron. Todos. Y nos acostamos. Cada uno fue a su lecho. Y dormimos, algunas horas, profundamente.

Y entre nosotros estaba el abuelo, muerto.

What a strange night when grandfather died. Drops of water, white pebbles, fell from the lemons and the rosebush. Out of the sideboard came rats; teacups by the dozen, always twelve, sherry glasses; the liquor in every color turned black.

Aunt Joseph screamed beside the body. The girls, every one of us, also screamed. Without warning, distant aunts appeared, cousins of cousins, suddenly, within a minute, as if they had traveled by horse or butterfly. And neighbors from the farthest farms, even the farms underground, came in their funeral carriages, full of watermelons.

I saw someone, very strange, in the mirror; I paid close attention in case it was a reflection; but no one there resembled him.

But at dawn the strangers departed. All of them. And we rested. Each of us went to her bed. And for a few hours we slept deeply.

And between us lay grandfather, dead.

Me vino un deseo misterioso de ver fruta, de comer fruta; y salí a la selva de la casa. Cacé una manzana, un membrillo malvarrosa, una ciruela y su capuchón azul. Asé, ligeramente, una dalia, y la comí, tragué una rosa; vi duraznos y su vino ocre, uvas rojas, negras, blancas; los higos, que albergan, por igual, al Diablo y a San Juan, y los racimos de bananas y de nísperos; me cayeron dátiles en la blusa.

Me crecieron alas, blanquísimas, me creció el vestido. Eché a volar. No quería volver, más. Llegué a un tejado; creyeron que era una cigüeña, un gran ángel; las mujeres gritaban; los hombres rondaron con intenciones ocultas.

No podía volver, ya.

Ando, ando.

Las gentes retornan de las fiestas, se desvelan;

y yo vuelvo a pasar volando.

I was struck by a strange desire to see fruit, to eat fruit; and I ran out of the house and into the forest. I caught an apple, a mauve-rose quince, a plum in its blue hood. I roasted, lightly, a dahlia, and ate it, I swallowed a rose; I saw peaches and their ocher wine, red, black, and white grapes; the figs that harbor equally the Devil and San Juan, and bunches of bananas and loquats; dates fell into my blouse.

I grew wings, milk-white; my dress grew. I took flight. I didn't want to go back, ever again. I came to a roof; they thought I was a stork, a great angel; the women were screaming; the men circled with dark designs.

I couldn't go back, now.

I go on, I go on.

The people come home from parties, they lie awake;

and I fly by.

Anoche, llegaron murciélagos.

Si no los llamo, ellos, igual, vienen.

Venían con las alas negras y el racimo.

Cayeron adentro de mi vestido blanco. De todas las rosas y camelias que he reunido en estos años. Y en la canasta de claveles y de fresias. La Virgen María dio un grito y atravesó todas las salas; con el pelo hasta el suelo y las dalias.

Las perlas, almendras y pastillas, las frutas de cristal y almíbar, que vivían en fruteras y cajas de porcelana, quedaron negras, y volvieron a ser claras, pero como muertas.

Yo me erguí. Goteaban sangre mi pañuelo blanco y mi garganta.

Last night, the bats came.

If I don't call to them, still, they come.

They came with black wings in a cluster.

They fell inside my white dress. Inside all the roses and camellias that I've gathered all these years. And in the basket of carnations and freesias. The Virgin Mary screamed and ran from room to room; her hair grazing the ground and the dahlias.

The pearls, almonds, and candy, the fruits of glass and syrup, which dwelled in fruit bowls and porcelain boxes, turned black, then clear again, but as if they were dead.

I stood up. Blood was dripping from my white handkerchief and my throat.

Hay caracoles, aquí y allá. Con sólo fijar la mirada, ya surgen.

Son de nácar, de azúcar y de loza; adentro, el pequeño monstruo rosado.

No sé si están inmóviles, caminan; arriba de las hojas de membrillo.

Y hay, también, quien caza caracoles, trae las canastitas; los cocina, los hierve, guardándoles las formas y los cuernos, los pone en fuentes y salseras. Y, entretanto, es Carnaval; anda toda la familia por la huerta, y los parientes más lejanos, los vecinos, conocidos, desconocidos. Los hombres parecen mujeres; las mujeres parecen hombres. No se sabe quién es quién. Todos usan delantales de flecos de colores, coronas, caravanas. Aquél va en una carroza con muchas lámparas. Se mueven, frenéticamente, escobas luminosas y sartenes.

Todos se han vuelto rosas o animales.

Los tíos más viejos y más serios, ahora, son estrellas o son zorros.

Y llueve, apenas, casi nada, dulcemente.

Y gente que no está en la fiesta, o que está —no se ve bien— saca, con cuidado, de las ramas, rosetas de brillantes, rositas, caracoles.

There are snails, here and there. If you simply fix your gaze, they appear.

They're made of mother-of-pearl, sugar, and china; and inside, the little pink monster.

I don't know if they stay in place, or walk; atop the leaves of the quince trees.

And the snail catchers are here too, with little baskets; they cook the snails, boil them, preserving their shapes and horns, put them on platters and in sauceboats. And, in the meantime, it's Carnaval; the whole family wanders through the garden, with our distant relatives, the neighbors whom we know, don't know. The men look like women; the women, like men. You can't tell who is who. They all wear pinafores with colorful fringes, tiaras, dangling earrings. That one there travels in a carriage with many lamps. Luminous brooms and pans shake back and forth.

They've all turned into roses or animals.

The oldest and gravest uncles, now, are stars or foxes.

And it's raining, just barely, as if it were nothing, gently.

And people who aren't part of the celebration, or who are—it's hard to tell—take carefully, from the branches, diamond rosettes, little roses, snails.

Al pasar me pareció que el árbol me llamaba, quería decirme algo. Me detuve; miré el tronco, largo, gris, un poco entreabierto arriba. Allí tenía metido un hongo, enorme, con un ala; parecía un animal o un sombrero, parecía una gallina. Eso era lo que quería avisarme el árbol. El hongo era gris, y a ratos, de un rosa morado. De tan rotundo, curvo, había echado hijos. En cualquier parte tenía numerosos muchachitos, huevos. Pude irme, entrar al bar; pero quedé. El árbol hablaba, me hablaba, sin hablar, que era su manera de hablar.

As I walked by, it seemed the tree was calling to me, wanting to tell me something. I stopped; I looked up at the large gray trunk, splitting at the top. There, tucked away, was a huge mushroom with a wing, it looked like an animal or hat, like a hen. That was what the tree wanted to tell me. The mushroom was gray, and at times, a purplish pink. It was so round, curved, it had sprouted children. It was covered with little boys and girls, eggs. I could have left, gone to the bar; but I stayed. The tree was speaking, speaking to me, without speaking, which was its way of speaking.

Al tornar del colegio, los otros niños jugaban en el patio; mamá preparó el té. Comencé a quitarme el delantal.

Enseguida, volvieron las plumas.

Mi rostro quedó absolutamente de perfil, se arqueó la nariz; crucé la ventana, volé al aire azul, batiendo las alas, blancas, pardas, grises, entreabiertas.

Bellísima, impresionante. El cuerpo era pequeño; parecía sólo una cabeza. Con desesperación recordé el lugar, el caminillo, el escondrijo. Llegué en un minuto; de un aletazo barrí el piso, la entrada, pulí los huevos, conté mis pollos; con miedo horrible de que no fuera a alcanzarme el tiempo salí a buscar presas; maté ratones de un picotazo en el oído; los distribuí; a cada uno, uno.

Torné de prisa, al aire azul. Pasó la muerte, tan delgada, con el vestido largo, blanco, de organdí. Entonces, di el grito petrificante que alertó a todo el valle. Y en el mismo momento, estuve, otra vez, de pie, en la otra casa. Mi madre recogía el delantal, servía el té, decía: "Gritó la lechuza".

After school, the other children played on the patio; mama made tea. I started to take off my pinafore.

Right away, the feathers returned.

My face was seen in strict profile, my nose arched; I flew out the window, into the blue air, beating my wings, white, brown, gray, unfurling.

Stunning, impressive. My body was small, as if it were only a head. Desperately, I remembered the site, the narrow path, the hiding place. I arrived in a minute; with a flick of the wing I swept the floor, the doorway, I polished the eggs, counted my chickens; with a horrible fear that I'd run out of time I went to search for prey; I killed mice with a peck to the ear; I divvied them up; one to each one.

I returned quickly, through the blue air. Death floated by, so thin, in her long white organdy dress. I let out a petrifying screech that warned the whole valley. And at the same time, I was standing again, in the other house. Mama was picking up my pinafore, pouring tea, saying, "The owl screeched."

Los "tucu-tucus", los topos de subtierra. Con los ojos ingenuos, aviesos, parecidos a los nuestros. Su familia y la nuestra habían vivido, desde tantos años, en el mismo sitio. Nosotros, en la casa de arriba; ellos, en la casa de abajo. Se comían las arvejillas, las raíces; pero de ellos, eran el cántico del atardecer, los tamboriles que decían, siempre, lo mismo, y daban un leve sobresalto.

Recuerdo a las novias de los huertos, cruzando las eras, para ir a casarse, vestidas de nieve y al compás de los escondidos tambores.

Y la luna pálida como un huevo (de las grandes lluvias); o la luna roja (de las sequías).

Y mi porvenir confuso, sin llegar a ningún sitio, salir del bosque, del negro canto. ¿Qué era eso que decían los topos, que yo no entendía?

The "tuco-tucos," the underground moles. With naive, cunning eyes, like our own. Their family and ours lived, for many years, in the same place. We, in the house above; they, in the house below. They ate the sweet peas, the roots; but from them came the evening hymn, the small drums that would, always, say the same thing, and cause a slight shudder.

I remember the brides of the orchards, crossing the garden beds, on their way to get married, dressed in snow, and in time with the hidden drums.

And the pale moon like an egg (in the heavy rains); or the red moon (in the droughts).

And my future uncertain, without arriving at any one place, leaving the forest, the dark song. What was it the moles said that I didn't understand?

Mi madre dijo: —En esta casa hay oculta una pierna. Y nada más dijo. Yo busqué en vano. A tontas y a locas. Pero cuando estuve enferma y con mucha fiebre, salí de la cama y abrí el ropero. Y hallé la pierna. Que no era gruesa ni delgada; parecía de hombre y de mujer. Tenía un zapato confuso y una media igual. Mamá apareció y completó el informe, dijo:

—Es una pierna de pollito.

Yo rememoré todos los pollitos que había visto en mi vida, de diversos colores, y todos tenían las patitas chicas y flaquitas. Clamé:

—De pollito?!

Mamá replicó: —Yo no miento. Odio a la mentira. La castigaría con la muerte.

Volví al lecho y me dormí y mejoré y sané.

Y no sabía de qué era la pierna, si estaba, si no estaba, no sabía dónde estaba.

My mother said, "There's a leg hidden in this house." And that was all she said. I searched in vain. Every which way. But when I was sick with a high fever, I got out of bed and opened the armoire. And came across the leg. Neither thick nor thin, it looked like a man's or woman's. It was wearing an odd shoe and sock. Mama appeared and filled in the particulars, she said:

"It's a baby chick's leg."

I thought back to all the chicks I'd seen in my life, of different colors, and they all had small, scrawny feet. I exclaimed:

"A baby chick?!"

Mama replied, "I don't lie. I detest lies. They should be punishable by death."

I went back to bed and slept and felt better and was cured.

And I didn't know what kind of leg it was, if it was there, if it wasn't, I didn't know where it was.

Cuando nació, apareció el lobo. Era un domingo al mediodía, –a las once y media, luz brillante–, y la madre vio a través del vidrio, el hocico picudo, y en la pelambre, las espinas de escarcha, y clamoreó; mas, le dieron una pócima que la adormecía alegremente.

El lobo asistió al bautismo y a la comunión; el bautismo, con faldones; la comunión, vestido rosa. El lobo no se veía; sólo asomaban sus orejas puntiagudas entre las cosas.

La persiguió a la escuela, oculto por rosales y repollos; la espiaba en las fiestas de exámenes, cuando ella tembló un poco.

Divisó al primer novio, y al segundo, y al tercero, que sólo la miraron tras la reja. Ella con el organdí ilusorio, que usaban entonces, las niñas de jardines. Y perlas, en la cabeza, en el escote, en el ruedo, perlas pesadas y esplendorosas, (era lo único que sostenía el vestido). Al moverse perdía alguna de esas perlas. Pero los novios desaparecieron sin que nadie supiese por qué.

Las amigas se casaban; unas tras otras; fue a las grandes fiestas; asistió al nacimiento de los niños de cada una.

Y los años pasaron y volaron, y ella en su extrañeza. Un día se volvió y dijo a alguien: Es el lobo.

Aunque en verdad ella nunca había visto un lobo.

Hasta que llegó una noche extraordinaria, por las camelias y las estrellas. Llegó una noche extraordinaria.

Detrás de la reja apareció el lobo; apareció como novio, como un hombre habló en voz baja y convincente. Le dijo: Ven. Ella obedeció; se le cayó una perla. Salió. Él dijo: –¿Acá?

Pero, atravesaron camelias y rosales, todo negro por la oscuridad, hasta un hueco que parecía cavado especialmente. Ella se arrodilló; él se arrodilló. Estiró su grande lengua y la lamió. Le dijo: ¿Cómo quieres?

Ella no respondía. Era una reina. Sólo la sonrisa leve que había visto a las amigas en las bodas.

Él le sacó una mano, y la otra mano; un pie, el otro pie; la contempló un instante así. Luego le sacó la cabeza; los ojos, (puso uno a cada lado); le sacó las costillas y todo.

Pero, por sobre todo, devoró la sangre, con rapidez, maestría y gran virilidad.

When she was born, the wolf appeared. It was a Sunday at noon—at eleven thirty, shining light—and her mother saw through the glass his long snout, and on his fur, frosty spikes, and cried out; but they gave her a concoction to drink that lulled her blissfully to sleep.

The wolf attended her baptism and her communion; the baptism, in a christening gown; the communion, a pink dress. No one saw the wolf; but his pointed ears poked out from under things.

He followed her to school, behind roses and cabbages; he spied on her during the parties after exams, when she felt a shiver.

He spotted her first boyfriend, and the second, and third, who only stared at her through the gate. She in the illusory organdy that girls in the gardens wore back then. And pearls, around her head, her neckline, her hem, heavy and luminous pearls, (they were the only thing that held up the dress). When she moved, she'd lose one of those pearls. But the boyfriends disappeared without anyone knowing why.

Her friends got married; one after the other; she went to the big parties; she was there when their children were born.

And the years flew and went, and she in her oddity. One day she turned and said to someone, "It's the wolf."

Although she'd never actually seen a wolf.

Until an extraordinary night arrived, among the camellias and the stars. An extraordinary night arrived.

Behind the gate the wolf appeared; he appeared like one of her boyfriends, like a man he spoke in a soft, convincing voice. He said, "Come." She obeyed; a pearl fell. She left. He said, "Here?"

But they walked through camellias and roses, black in the darkness, to a hole that seemed to have been dug for a reason. She knelt down; he knelt down. He stretched out his long tongue and licked her. He said, "How do you want it?"

She wouldn't answer. She was a queen. Only the faint smile that she'd seen on her friends at their weddings.

He pulled out her hand, the other hand; a foot, the other foot; he considered her for a moment like that. Then he pulled off her head; pulled out her eyes, (set one to each side); her ribs, and all.

But, above all, he devoured her blood, with speed, skill, and great virility.

Uno de los huevos que puso mamá era rosado bellísimo; se entreabrió al final de la primavera con un murmullo de papeles acresponados. De él salieron hombres y mujeres, de ya neto perfil, zorras, arañas, alondras —todo creciendo rápidamente—, hierbecitas, moluscos, un hada con una dalia granate en la mano.

Eso estaba unido y se desunía y volvía a unirse, acaso con temor de la luz.

La primera en liberarse fue una zorra, que huyó hacia los matorrales; tenía un colgaje; había nacido con adorno, que mamá ordenó quitarse, no sé por qué; ella no hizo caso, y chapoteaba en los pequeños laureles.

Yo quería enumerar todo lo que había nacido.

Mamá estaba alta y erguida. A ratos, echaba una mirada a la cáscara rota, color rosa, de la que seguían apareciendo murciélagos y mariposas.

One of the eggs that mother laid was the most beautiful shade of pink; it began to hatch at the end of spring with a rustling of ruffled paper. Men and women emerged, already with distinct profiles, foxes, spiders, larks—everything springing up quickly—sprouts of grass, mollusks, a fairy with a crimson dahlia in its hand.

It was all conjoined and would disjoin and rejoin, afraid perhaps of the light.

The first one to break free was a fox, who took off toward the bushes; she wore a pendant; she'd been born with adornment, which mama ordered her to remove, I'm not sure why; the fox ignored her, and splashed about in the small bay laurels.

I wanted to list everything that had been born.

Mama stood tall and straight. Now and then, she'd shoot a glance at the cracked pink shell—bats and butterflies still streaming out.

Cuando fui de visita al altar usé vestido de organdí celeste más largo que yo, por donde, a ratos, sobresalía un pie de oro, tan labrado y repujado, desde el seno mismo de mi madre! Mi pelo también era de organza celeste, más largo que el vestido, pero podía pasar al rosa y aun al pálido topacio.

Desde que llegué las habitantes se pusieron a rezar, y así empezó la novela, la novena empezó así. Los picaflores, colibríes, atravesaban las oraciones; entraban a ellas y salían; su fugaz presencia produjo, primero, desasosiego, para dar después otras destreza e intensidad a la sagrada murmuración.

Algunos seres estuvieron de visita, afuera y por un segundo; vino la Vaca de cara triste; el Conejo, la Nieve y una mosca.

Mientras estuve, las habitantes rezaron apasionadamente, mirando sin cesar, mi velo, mi pelo, que en pocos segundos, iba del azul al rosa y aun al rubí pálido, con absoluta naturalidad.

When I visited the altar I wore a sky-blue organdy dress longer than my legs, under which, now and then, a gold foot would poke out, finely wrought and embossed, from my mother's own womb! My hair was also sky-blue organza, longer than the dress, but it could turn pink and even light topaz.

The moment I arrived, the women inside started to pray, and like that the novel began, the novena began like that. Hummingbirds fluttered through the prayers; they flew in and out of them; their ever-shifting presence was, at first, disquieting, to then add to the skill and ardor of the sacred murmuring.

Some creatures were visiting, outside for a second; the sad-faced Cow showed up; the Rabbit, the Snow, and a fly.

While I stood there, the women prayed with fervor, staring incessantly at my veil, my hair, which every few seconds turned from blue to pink and even light ruby, quite naturally.

Gilberto, el paragüero, vendía paraguas, sólo en los días de lluvia. Nunca bajo el sol ofreció su mercancía. En el libro de la escuela figuraba Gilberto el paragüero!

Y me habían enseñado la "tabla del dos"; vine alborozada con esa adquisición científica. La maestra era una sabia. Se llamaba María-Esther.

Cantaron las calandrias, cantaron las "ladronas" (esas urracas); de pie, en el alambre y entre la ropa, estaban las pajarracas.

Llovía dulcemente sobre los claveles, sobre las viejas cacerolas tiradas en el jardín, en las que bullían hongos de diversos tamaño y forma, blanca hierba y caracoles –tenebrosos– blancos como el azúcar y la sal.

Compré –a Gilberto– para pasearme, un paraguas con todos los colores, y un par de zapatos, igual.

Gilberto, the umbrella vender, would sell umbrellas only on days when it rained. He never peddled his wares in the sunshine. In the schoolbook appeared Gilberto the umbrella vender!

And they had taught me the "two times table"; I was thrilled to acquire that bit of science. The teacher was a sage. Her name was Maria-Esther.

The larks sang, the "thieves" sang (those magpies); on the line between our clothes perched those black spies.

It would rain softly on the carnations, on the old pots lying in the garden, which teemed with mushrooms of different shapes and sizes, pale grass, and snails—shadowy—pale as sugar and salt.

I bought—from Gilberto—to take on a stroll, a rainbow-colored umbrella, and a pair of shoes to match.

En la habitación oscura, sin abrir la puerta, alguien entró, y comenzó a peinarme. Yo, singularmente, apenas me defendía.

Me peinaba hebra por hebra, a todo lo largo, y hacía cerquillos, bucles, rizos, y nuevamente a todo lo largo. El peine era opaco, y a ratos con un esplendor de coral.

Yo, casi nada efectuaba por librarme, hasta que el pelo quedó tendido y lacio, y su punta tocaba el suelo y seguía como un río.

Y quien me peinó desapareció en la oscuridad –sin abrir la puerta– así como había venido.

In the dark room, without opening the door, someone entered, and began to comb my hair. I, for some reason, barely resisted.

Strand by strand, the comb swept through my hair, down to the ends, and made bangs, ringlets, curls, and swept down to the ends again. The comb was opaque, and sometimes as lustrous as coral.

I, hardly tried to escape, until my hair hung loose and straight, and its tips touched the floor and kept flowing like a river.

And whatever had combed my hair disappeared into the darkness— without opening the door—as it had come.

Hacía tiempo que estaban esperando el Alma. Y el Alma nunca venía. Mamá hizo golosinas de colores y las guardó en cajas negras, y en un plato colocaba velas de diversos tamaño y forma. ¿Y cómo sería el Alma? ¿Los pies de oro y plata? ¿Coronas de cristal? ¿Tejida en hilo blanco igual a un tul? ¿Jazmines en vez de huesos?

Para aguardarla pusieron rosales en todo la pradera y gladiolos como un mar. Había una nave entre la hierba, y las ratas reinaban sobre el mar (rosado y breve de las huertas).

Pero el Alma se negaba a aparecer.

¡Hasta que quedó sentada entre nosotros súbitamente en un atardecer!

Las estrellas caían, a tontas y locas, como arvejas y maíz; la nave campesina llegó junto a la ventana y su velamen ensombreció todo; los gladiolos quisieron salvarse y huían hacia el sur; pero en mitad, ya fríos, murieron y crujieron.

Cada uno de los habitantes de la casa se puso a gritar; pero, no, juntos, (y esto fue lo raro), sino por turno.

Yo fui la última en gritar y sin querer toqué una mano del Alma, que tenía muchísimos dedos, muchísimos, como pistilos, como cien.

El Alma me miró y se fue.

For a long time they awaited the Soul. And the Soul never came. Mama made colorful candies and stored them in dark boxes, and on a plate she arranged candles of different shapes and sizes. What would the Soul be like? Gold and silver feet? Crystal crowns? Woven with white thread like tulle? Jasmine instead of bones?

In anticipation they planted rosebushes throughout the meadow and a sea of gladioli. A boat lay in the grass, and the rats reigned over the sea (the brief pink sea of the gardens).

But the Soul refused to appear.

Until it was sitting there suddenly among us one evening!

The stars were falling, every which way, like peas and corn; the country boat was blown against the window and its sails cast a shadow over everything; the gladioli tried to save themselves and fled south; but along the way, freezing, they died and creaked.

Everyone in the house started to scream; but not all at once, (and this was the strange part), but one by one.

I was the last to scream and by accident I touched one of the Soul's hands, which had many fingers, so many, like pistils, almost a hundred.

The Soul looked at me and left.

Cuando nací mamá se dio cuenta de que yo era una mariposa. Y con un punzón, que ya tendría preparado, o que sacó de la caja de objetos prodigiosos, me traspasó tan diestramente, que quedé viva, y, así, me puso en el cuadro de sus postales más hermosas. Con el tiempo mis alas aumentaron y cambiaban los colores, celestes y rosados. Hasta tuve una orla color plata, color oro, y puntitos, igual. Mis antenas se iban como hilos, por el olor de las rosas del jardín, los jazmines y azaleas, y brillantes del rocío.

Pero, mamá no dejaba de mirarme. Aunque estuviese en la cocina con las habas y el cuchillo, en el huerto, en el altar, con mi padre, o sus hermanas.

Jamás sacó los ojos de su hija mariposa. No quitó el punzón que me separaba de las rosas.

When I was born mama realized that I was a butterfly. And with a thick pin, which she must have set out ahead of time, or took from the chest of wondrous objects, she pierced through me so deftly that I stayed alive, and she pinned me like that to the collage of her prettiest postcards. In time, my wings widened and changed colors, sky blue and pink. I even grew a border of silver, of gold, with matching spots. My antennae would straighten like threads, from the smell of the roses in the garden, the jasmine and azaleas, and gems of dew.

But mama always watched me. Whether she was in the kitchen with the fava beans and knife, in the orchard, at the altar, with my father, or her sisters.

She never lifted her eyes off her butterfly daughter. She didn't remove the pin that kept me from the roses.

El Día de los Muertos los árboles se ponen muy simples, como hojas; les recorre una luz azul.

Los muertos aparecen, acostados, o de rodillas, intentan andar. Uno echa una mirada erótica hacia una muerta rubia que sobresale más allá.

Pero, enseguida comienza a hacer frío. El sol queda negro, sólo con la "sortija", la hilacha; los pájaros pían y se van al nido.

Una oveja se acuesta de espaldas; con los pies para arriba.

Y lo que es de abajo torna a bajar.

On the Day of the Dead the trees become very plain, like leaves; a blue light passes through them.

The dead appear, lying down, or on their knees, and try to walk. One glances leeringly at a dead blonde who stands out from afar.

But right away it starts to get cold. The sun goes black, leaving only a ring, a raveled thread; birds chirp and fly to the nest.

A sheep lies on its back; with its hooves in the air.

And what's from below begins again to lower.

Acknowledgments

Translation is, by definition, a collaboration, and I am indebted not only to Marosa di Giorgio, but to numerous others who provided assistance during the compilation of this book. I would like to thank Wilka Roig, who carefully read and commented on the manuscript; Katherine Larson, for her wholehearted enthusiasm and help with the arrangement of the book; David Young and Martha Collins, my former professors at Oberlin College, who fostered my interest in translation and offered advice on this manuscript. Thanks also to Sebastian Faber, Steven Hess, Patrick O'Connor, Ana Cara, Silvia Alvarez Olarra, Jorge Rosario-Vélez, and Sonia Lugo for discussing some of these poems with me and offering advice.

I was fortunate to travel to Uruguay for several weeks while completing the book, and am grateful to di Giorgio's family and friends, who shared their reminiscences and insights with me, especially her sister, Nidia di Giorgio, and niece, Jazmín Lacoste di Giorgio, who greeted me with warmth. I am also indebted to Roberto Echavarren, Luis Bravo, Marisa Canut Guevara, and Hebert Benítez Pezzolano for sharing with me their expertise on di Giorgio, and to Leonardo Garet and Myriam Albisu, my ambassadors to Salto, who brought me to what remains of the di Giorgio family farm.

In addition, I am grateful to the editors of *Mantis, Subtropics, New American Writing, Washington Square, Pleiades, Hanging Loose, Field,* and *Iowa Review,* where some of these translations first appeared; to Adriana Hidalgo, Ana Skiendziel, and the rest of the staff at Adriana Hidalgo Editora for their assistance; to Rusty Morrison and Ken Keegan for their interest in the project; to María Negroni for discussing some of the translations during a workshop at McNally Jackson Books; to Carol Fishwick for lending her expertise on flowers; to Barbara Weissberger, who generously provided the cover art; to the Lannan Foundation for supporting this translation; and, most importantly, to Peter Conners and the staff at BOA Editions for believing in me and shepherding this book into your hands.

Finally, I would like to thank my family for their love and patience.

About the Author

"I always felt Italian and South American at the same time. The place where the first thirteen years of my life transpired was like Tuscany transplanted," claimed Marosa di Giorgio in an interview. Descended from Italian immigrants of Tuscan origin, she was born in 1932 in the city of Salto in northwestern Uruguay, and was raised with a strong Catholic faith outside of the city in an area devoted to farming. The family moved to the center of the city when di Giorgio entered high school at the age of thirteen. She published her first book, *Poemas* (Poems), in 1953. In the 1950s and 60s she was devoted to the theater and participated as an actress in almost thirty productions in works by Jacinto Benavente, Alexandre Dumas, Florencio Sánchez, Gabriel Marcel, and Noël Coward, among others. From 1957 to 1962, she was in charge of the society and culture section of a local newspaper, and then worked for the government in an administrative position. In 1978, after the death of her father, the family relocated to Montevideo, where she lived until she died of bone cancer in 2004. While living in Montevideo, she would frequent the city's cafés—particularly Café Sorocabana in Plaza Cagancha—where invariably she could be seen sipping coffee or wine, or conversing with other writers and painters. She never married or had children.

Di Giorgio expanded the same work throughout her career: *Los papeles salvajes* (The Wild Papers, 2008), her collected poetry, which unites fourteen books. Since her poems inhabit the same imaginative world, they can be read as one long meditation, which di Giorgio described as a forest in which she planted more trees. The first edition was published in 1971, gathering together her first seven books, and then expanded over the course of her lifetime. In 2008, Adriana Hidalgo, an editorial house in Buenos Aires, published the collection posthumously in one single volume. Di Giorgio also composed three books of erotic tales—which were recently collected in *El gran ratón dorado, el gran ratón de las lilas* (The Great Golden Mouse, the Great Mouse of Lilacs, 2008)—and a novel, *Reina Amelia* (Queen Amelia, 1999). Completed shortly before her death, her final book, *La flor de lis* (Fleur de Lis, 2004), combines narrative and lyric modes, synthesizing her life's work.

She received several awards throughout her career, including a Fulbright Scholarship and, in 2001, First Prize in the International Poetry Festival in Medellín. Drawing on her background in theater, she gave dramatic recitals of her poems, and traveled as far as France to give performances. Her work has previously been translated into English in *The History of Violets* (Ugly Duckling, 2010) and *Hotel Lautreamont: Contemporary Poetry from Uruguay* (Shearsman, 2011).

About the Translator

Adam Giannelli is a graduate of Oberlin College and the University of Virginia, where he was a Hoyns Fellow in the MFA program. His poems and translations have appeared in *New England Review, Kenyon Review, Field, Colorado Review, New American Writing, Two Lines, The FSG Book of Twentieth-Century Italian Poetry*, and elsewhere. He is the editor of a book of critical essays: *High Lonesome: On the Poetry of Charles Wright* (Oberlin College Press, 2006).

The Lannan Translations Selection Series

Ljuba Merlina Bortolani, *The Siege*

Olga Orozco, *Engravings Torn from Insomnia*

Gérard Martin, *The Hiddenness of the World*

Fadhil Al-Azzawi, *Miracle Maker*

Sándor Csoóri, *Before and After the Fall: New Poems*

Francisca Aguirre, *Ithaca*

Jean-Michel Maulpoix, *A Matter of Blue*

Willow, Wine, Mirror, Moon: Women's Poems from Tang China

Felipe Benítez Reyes, *Probable Lives*

Ko Un, *Flowers of a Moment*

Paulo Henriques Britto, *The Clean Shirt of It*

Moikom Zeqo, *I Don't Believe in Ghosts*

Adonis (Ali Ahmad Sa'id), *Mihyar of Damascus, His Songs*

Maya Bejerano, *The Hymns of Job and Other Poems*

Novica Tadić, *Dark Things*

Praises & Offenses: Three Women Poets of the Dominican Republic

Ece Temelkuran, *Book of the Edge*

Aleš Šteger, *The Book of Things*

Nikola Madzirov, *Remnants of Another Age*

Carsten René Nielsen, *House Inspections*

Jacek Gutorow, *The Folding Star and Other Poems*

Marosa di Giorgio, *Diadem*

For more on the Lannan Translations Selection Series
visit our website:
www.boaeditions.org

9 781934 414972